SECOND EDITION

HUMAN BEHAVIOR

A Perspective for the Helping Professions

ROBERT L. BERGER
Thomas More College

RONALD C. FEDERICO
Iona College

Longman
New York & London

HUMAN BEHAVIOR
A Perspective for the Helping Professions, 2nd Edition.

Longman Inc., 95 Church Street, White Plains, N.Y. 10601
Associated companies, branches, and representatives
throughout the world.

Developmental Editor: Irving E. Rockwood
Editorial and Design Supervisor: Barbara Lombardo
Design: Gloria Moyer
Cover Photograph: Margarita Lopez (top right and left),
    Barbara Lombardo (bottom right)

Library of Congress Cataloging in Publication Data

Berger, Robert, 1937-
   Human behavior, a perspective for the helping
professions.

   Rev. ed. of: Human behavior, a social work perspective.
c1982.
   Bibliography: p.
   Includes index.
   1. Social case work. 2. Human behavior. I. Federico,
Ronald C. II. Berger, Robert, 1937-   . Human
behavior, a social work perspective. III. Title.
HV43.B45 1985   361.3'2   84-14416
ISBN 0-582-28521-6 (pbk.)

Manufactured in the United States of America
Printing: 9 8 7   Year: 92 91 90 89

CONTENTS

PREFACE

This book is about what is most important to people, and how these things affect their lives. Many factors influence what people view as important and attainable. Some of these factors are concrete. For example, some people who lack formal education find themselves excluded from desirable jobs and reluctantly give up their dream of work that is interesting and rewarding. Other factors are more intangible, but are nevertheless real. Religious beliefs may support a dream that people can get along without racial conflict even though such conflict presently occurs. To understand people's lives, we must understand the hopes and wishes that lead them to act as they do. These may themselves be rather abstract in the minds of the people who cherish them. However, the factors that shape them are very specific and can be studied with some degree of precision. The goals of this book, then, are to help you understand why people have their dreams, how their behavior is affected by them, and how they get modified and sometimes destroyed.

Helping professionals are in the business of enabling people to attain their life goals. We must first understand what is of value to people because values and goals are closely related. People seek what they value, and act in ways which are consistent with their values. Professional helpers must also understand what people consider appropriate strategies to attain their goals. Understanding, of course, requires knowledge. Because the factors that influence people's dreams and values are of many kinds, the knowledge needed is diversified and extensive. This book will help you review the knowledge that you already have and, when necessary, to aquire useful new knowledge. But an additional important goal of this book is to assist you to learn how to *use* your knowledge as a professional helping person. Unlike scientists, who seek knowledge in order to better understand human behavior and phenomena in the natural world, helping professionals use knowledge to help others. As you move through this book, we will help you to develop skill in knowledge application.

In many cases, the helping professional must first help people to articulate their values and goals. These may be deeply held, but rarely made explicit in thought or speech. When people are helped to examine and express their values and goals, they sometimes decide to modify them, or see more clearly various strategies for attaining them. Effective helping involves planning *with* others, not *for* them. Participating in planning means being able to understand what people want and finding ways of attaining it. Of course, people may want things that are impossible for them to have. In these cases, acknowledging this reality with sensitivity and interpersonal support is part of what the helping professional brings to the process.

Let's stop at this point and look at some examples. We often read in the newspapers stories of people who exhibit great courage and even heroism. In these cases it is very clear how a dearly held goal is motivating behavior. For example, an athelete who accepts a rigorous training routine in order to compete in the Olympics is making sacrifices to attain an important goal. Someone who risks his/her own life to save someone else's is also seeking a goal. In this case the goal, to help another human being, is closely tied to values respecting human life and accepting one's own responsibility for preserving and nuturing it. This same insight helps us to understand very different situtions, as well. People who turn their backs on others have defined their own survival, success, or comfort as their most important goal. Even those who engage in self-destructive behavior are expressing their sense of priorities and their values. For some, facing economic loss, the loss of a loved one, or the trauma of an illness or emotional crisis may be so overwhelming that death is seen as preferable to life. This is especially likely when people feel cut off from others who care about them. And some people do not understand how their behaviors may be leading them away from their goals, rather than toward them as they had hoped.

The hopes and wishes that motivate behavior are many and often contradictory. Parents may envision their children becoming economically successful, yet also want them to be caring, honest people who are ethical and not too aggressive. Other parents also dream of economic well-being for their offspring, but do not know how to educate or otherwise prepare them so that the goal is likely to be attained. Still other parents have the same dream, but have also come to believe that the reality of their lives makes it unrealistic. As a result, they may actively discourage their children from pursuing such a goal. We all have hopes and related goals for ourselves and others. It is sometimes difficult to establish workable priorities among them, and to sort out those that are likely to be attainable from those that are not. Professional helpers assist people as they express, clarify, and organize their dreams and goals.

The task of understanding what is important to people and the strategies that they choose to attain their goals is a very difficult one. Human behavior is made up of many factors operating in interaction. The result is a rich but complex network of interactions. Involved in this network are inividuals; groups of people, such as friends and family members; organizations, such as social agencies and businesses; communities; and the larger structures that constitute society as a whole. Because all of these levels of interaction have to be understood, this book will attempt to lead you through each.

Lest you become discouraged by the magnitude of the task, keep in mind that you already know a great deal about human behavior. In the courses you have taken in the humanities, anthropology, psychology, sociology, political science, economics, and biology, you have learned much about various facets of people and their behavior. Building on this, the focus in this book will be on helping you to review what you know, learn some techniques for integrating that broad range of knowledge, and then develop skill in applying it to real-life situations that helping people commonly encounter. The end result of your using this book, then, should be very practical. You should be more confident about what you know, and you should be able to use your knowledge to help yourself and others.

OBJECTIVES

This book is intended to enable helping professionals to utilize knowledge in their practice. By understanding human behavior in its social context, helping professionals can make practice decisions more effectively. Several assumptions underlie this point of view:

1. Knowledge is fundamental for professionally responsible helping efforts.

2. Some knowledge is more useful for practice than other knowledge. In particular, knowledge that establishes a systems and human diversity context for human behavior is most useful for understanding situations in which people need or want help.

3. In order to be useful for practice, knowledge (in the form of concepts and data) must be learned, interrelated, and applied to actual life situations. The practitioner must also know how to determine which concepts and data are most useful in specific practice situations.

4. The current state of our knowledge does not allow us to understand all human behavior. We encourage the reader to maintain a sense of awe and wonderment when confronted with the complexities of human behavior. At the same time, this book will try to illuminate as much human behavior and the richness of its social context as our present knowledge makes possible.

The book's three principle objectives derive from the above assumptions. These objectives are the following:

1. *To systematically review and summarize concepts and data that have particular relevance for practice.* Useful concepts have been developed by various disciplines in the biological, social, and behavioral sciences. In the book, concepts will be drawn primarily from sociology, pychology, political science, economics, anthropology, and (human) biology. In addition to summarizing selected concepts, the book will discuss their utility for practice.

2. *To develop a framework that can be used to integrate the concepts relevant to understanding human behavior.* While individual disciplines concentrate on the teaching of discrete concepts and theories, this book will focus on finding relationships among them. This will make it

easier to perceive and understand human behavior as a totality rather than as discrete, or separate, actions.

3. *To demonstrate how integrated knowledge may be used by helping professionals.* In support of this objective, we will seek to establish a context for the analysis and decision making that are essential components of practice.

FEATURES OF THIS EDITION

In comparison with the previous edition, this one incorporates a great deal more illustrative and case material. This edition also addresses the linkage between knowledge and practice more specifically and explicitly. Each chapter has one or more exhibits that provide a realistic look at the lives of people. These exhibits illustrate what is discussed in the text, and also provide the opportunity to begin applying what has been learned. This edition also offers an overview at the beginning of each chapter. This will help to show how the pieces of the book fit together by highlighting the most significant issues. As with the last edition, each chapter also has a summary and study questions at the end. These should help in assessing whether the content of the chapter has been learned, and whether application to the "real world" is possible. A final new feature in this edition is a list of key terms at the end of each chapter that will help in the review of major concepts used in the book. An index is provided so that topics for review can be located when desired.

Another change in this edition is its length. It is longer than the first edition. This results in part from the greater emphasis on providing examples and case materials. It also reflects some reorganization of the material to make it clearer as well as to make the linkage between knowledge and practice much more explicit. This should make it far easier to relate this book to practice courses as well as specific practice activities; especially assessment. The increased length also means that the "outline" quality of the first edition has been reduced. The book flows more easily, is more interesting, and addresses the concepts in a more useful way. All in all, it is hoped that this edition is both more useful and more fun to read.

ACKNOWLEDGMENTS

Many people have contributed to this revision. A person whose contribution is very visible is Dr. Dee Thornberry at Madonna College in Livonia, Michigan. She generously developed and shared a set of illustrations to help explain the concepts in the book. Many other students and educators around the country have contributed their reactions to the first edition, and made suggestions for this edition. These have been extremely helpful in revising the book. Similarly, colleagues and students in our own schools have made valuable and useful suggestions. We appreciate these contributions very much; the book as it is would not have been possible without them.

As with any book, the publisher's role has also been significant in this revision. First, their confidence has encouraged and helped sustain us. In particular, the confidence of Lane Akers and Irving Rockwood has been especially supportive. Second, the expert editorial and production assistance has been of critical importance. David Estrin and Barbara Lombardo have overseen the production process, attending to the countless details which were important for making this book a reality. They, in turn, have had the help of Gloria Moyer in designing the book, and Hal Keith for doing the art work which illustrates points made in the text. To these colleagues, as well as the numerous others who have helped in some way, we express our sincere appreciation and gratitude.

The authors and publisher also gratefully acknowledge permission to reprint the following:

"Veronica's Short, Sad Life—Prostitution at 11, Death at 12," from *The New York Times*, October 3, 1977. Copyright© 1977 by The New York Times Company. Reprinted by permission.

"Aggression: Still a Stronger Trait for Males," from *The New York Times*, June 20, 1983. Copyright© 1983 by The New York Times Company. Reprinted by permission.

"Put Out to Pasture: Our Idea of Age 65," from *The New York Times*, February 7, 1984. Copyright© 1984 by The New York Times Company. Reprinted by permission.

"Crime at an Early Age: The Violent Streets of Luis Guzman," from *The New York Times*, November 9, 1981. Copyright© 1981 by The New York Times Company. Reprinted by permission.

"Family Tries with Welfare to 'Make Do'," from *The New York Times*, March 23, 1982. Copyright© 1982 by The New York Times Company. Reprinted by permission.

"Child Abuse Cases: Broken Homes, Teen-Age Parents, Drugs, and Death," from *The New York Times*, May 1, 1984. Copyright© 1984 by The New York Times Company. Reprinted by permission.

"The Victors" from *The New York Times Magazine*, January 29, 1984. Copyright© 1984 by Curtis Bill Pepper. Reprinted by permission of the Julian Bach Literary Agency, Inc. and The New York Times Company.

Excerpts from "Man-O-Pause: The Climateric in Men," from *Medical Self-Care*, Winter 1981. Copyright© 1981 by *Medical Self-Care Magazine*. Reprinted by permission.

Excerpts from *American Hunger Crisis*. Copyright© 1984 by Citizen's Commision on Hunger in New England. Reprinted by permission.

Excerpt from *Adulthood and Aging: An Interdisciplinary Developmental View* by Douglas C. Kimmel. Copyright© 1980 by John Wiley & Sons, Inc. Reprinted by permission.

1

HUMAN BEHAVIOR AND EFFECTIVE PRACTICE

CHAPTER OVERVIEW

This chapter focuses on the reasons why knowledge is important for effective professional helping. A model of generalist practice (based on social work) is adopted after showing how this approach also provides a useful foundation for helping professionals who practice as specialists. The linkage between professional purposes and the knowledge needed to carry out those purposes is described. Generalist helping is shown to focus on the mobilization and use of resources to help people define and meet their needs. A set of competencies to do this is discussed, followed by an overview of the day-to-day practice activities that flow from the competencies. These activities are in turn organized into a problem-solving model. Holistic assessment as a part of problem solving is particularly emphasized. This chapter, then, lays the foundation for the rest of the book by clarifying the purposes of professional helping. A sense of professional purpose then becomes the framework for deciding what kind of knowledge is especially useful for practice. This is the knowledge that is reviewed, integrated, and applied in the remainder of the book.

COMMITMENT, SKILL, AND KNOWLEDGE IN PRACTICE

A central task of professional helpers is to assist people and systems to function more effectively so that they can attain their goals with as few obstacles and as little pain as possible (Federico, 1984, chap. 1). Doing this involves the use of many resources, among the most important of which are characteristics of the helping person him/herself. Two are especially important: commitment and knowledge (Federico, 1984, chap. 4). Without the basic commitment to help others there is neither the desire nor drive to struggle with the complexities of effective helping. The day-to-day effort to help people who are enmeshed in difficult and often painful situations yields rewards only to those who are committed to this task (Konle, 1982).

Motivated by a solid commitment to help others, and assuming the ability to relate effectively to others, the helping professional also needs knowledge. Human behavior is rich and complex. Many factors are involved in any life situation; this is especially true in situations requiring professional help. Efforts to provide help must grow out of the ability to accurately understand problematic situations and the resources and obstacles that are embedded in them (Berelson and Steiner, 1964; Smalley, 1967; Zimbalist, 1977). No matter how committed a helping professional may be, knowledge is needed to effectively help others. On the other hand, knowledge alone is not sufficient. It must be used in a caring and ethical way on behalf of others, and it must be supported by effective helping skills. Exhibit 1.1, at the end of this chapter, illustrates the interplay of commitment, skill, and knowledge. In the case described there, no one seemed to have the necessary commitment to follow through on the many problems with which a young girl, Veronica, and her family were struggling. Veronica was also never engaged in a helping relationship that was managed with enough skill to keep her involved. Finally, knowledge of her total situation was lacking so that no helper understood fully what was happening to her and what needed to be done. Lacking adequate help and intervention on her behalf, Veronica became a prostitute at 11 and was dead at 12.

ISSUES IN SELECTING KNOWLEDGE: SPECIALISTS AND GENERALISTS

Given that knowledge is needed for effective helping, we must now address the question of *what* knowledge. We live in a world that sees almost daily breakthroughs in new knowledge areas: microelectronics, genetic engineering, laser technology, chemical analysis, and so on. What knowledge is of particular relevance to professional helping? First, we have to recognize that *all knowledge* may affect professional helping. For example, advances in microelectronics have created computers which are very useful for record-keeping in social welfare agencies. They have created changes in the workplace that have had profound effects on the family and on people's sense of well-being. In addition, they have had a ripple effect in other parts of the social world, such as school and transportation systems. Microelectronics, therefore, cannot be ignored, yet neither is an in-depth knowledge of it needed by most professional helpers. Instead, they should know how to use relevant products of microelectronic technology (like computers), and seek to understand the human needs created by this rapidly expanding part of our social system.

Making decisions regarding relevant and useful knowledge results from our sense of the purposes as professional helpers. We must be able to state what they do in order to identify the knowledge that will help them to do it. Up until now we have been talking about professional helpers as a group, but there are many categories of professional helpers: doctors and teachers, social workers and nurses, psychotherapists and physical therapists, police officers and gerontologists, and many others. Can we say that the purposes of each group are the same? Yes and no.

Understanding similarities and differences among professional helpers requires that we look at two types of professional helping: specialized helping and generalist helping. A **specialist** provides specific kinds of helping services in particular types of situations. For example, a surgeon performs surgery on people who have certain kinds of illnesses, and a police officer intervenes in situations where violations of law occur. Specialized training and knowledge are needed to provide specialized services. None of us would entrust our body to a surgeon who had not had special training to perform the kind of surgery we needed.

The **generalist,** on the other hand, addresses the needs of the whole person, and tries to find the package of resources that will address the range of needs that people have. Someone requiring surgery may simply need a competent surgeon. S/he may have sufficient money to pay for the surgery and hospitalization, a supportive family that will provide emotional support and maintain the patient's home environment while s/he is hospitalized, and so on. Others who undergo surgery may need help locating a competent surgeon, paying for the medical care they receive, dealing with their fears of surgery, maintaining relationships with friends or family, caring for their home while they are hospitalized, and so forth. The generalist responds to multiple levels of need—simply linking a patient with a surgeon in the first example, or attending to the whole range of needs in the second example.

Kahn and Kamerman (1976, p. 369) identify the following as the basic function of the generalist helper:

1. Giving information and advice and making referrals about all of the social sector (human services, in the broadest sense)

2. Giving access to a range of social-care services that enable handicapped, frail elderly, and disturbed people to remain in the community, living under some protection and with needed services and resources

3. Providing front-line counseling, if only on a simple level

4. Coping with emergency daytime, after-hour, and weekend needs for housing, food, protection, institutionalization for the vulnerable aged, children, and mentally ill, and others—whether directly or by access to other community service personnel

5. Carrying out appropriate ongoing treatment, including efforts in individualized, group, and residential contexts to bring about changes in adjustment, functioning, and view of self or others

6. Providing case integration, assuring that sequential service—that is, work with different family members within the personal-general social services or between programs in different systems—is mutually supportive and properly meshed

From the above, it becomes clear that generalists work at many levels—with individuals, with families and other groups of people, with agencies and other organizations, and with communities.

Specialists and generalists, then, address different dimensions of helping. Yet they work together. As the generalist puts together resources to help people deal with the range of needs they have, various specialists may be contacted. In our example of the person requiring surgery, the generalist might contact many helping professionals: a surgeon, social workers who could link the patient with financial assistance to handle the medical costs, psychiatrists who could help with the fears and disrupted personal relationships being encountered, and so on. Specialists should be aware of how their specialized service fits into the overall life of the patient, so that the doctor is not unwittingly increasing fear of medical treatment while the therapist is trying to reduce it. Similarly, the doctor's decision about when the patient is ready to be released should be made in conjunction with other helping professionals who have information about the home situation.

It is worthwhile to recall at this point that the discussion of specialists and generalists resulted from the need to clarify helping purposes in order to identify relevant knowledge needed to carry them out. We have seen that the purposes of specialists and generalists are somewhat different. Therefore, the knowledge they need is different. However, we have also seen that specialists and generalists have to work together so that optimal help is provided for all aspects of problematic life situations. The approach taken in this book will be to focus on the work of the generalist. This is obviously most relevant to generalists, but it is also important to specialists because it will enable them to relate their helping efforts to those of the generalists who are managing the total helping situation. What will be covered in this book provides a foundation for specialists. They may build on this foundation when they go on to acquire greater in-depth knowledge in areas of special relevance for their particular practice activities.

The approach to generalist practice taken in this book is borrowed from the field of social work. Social work is a profession that has made much progress in developing a clearly articulated model of generalist practice. However, you should keep in mind that most of the knowledge presented is relevant to any professional generalist helper. Furthermore, the linkage between knowledge and practice that will be described is also appropriate for all generalist helpers.

THE PURPOSES OF GENERALIST
SOCIAL WORK PRACTICE

Baer and Federico (1978, p. 68) define the purposes of **generalist social work practice** as follows:

Social work is concerned and involved with the interactions between people and the institutions of society that affect the ability of people to accomplish life tasks, realize aspirations and values, and alleviate distress. These interactions between people and social institutions occur within the context of the larger societal good. Therefore, three major purposes of social work may be identified:

1. to enhance the problem-solving, coping, and developmental capacities of people;
2. to promote the effective and humane operation of the systems that provide people with resources, services, and opportunities;
3. to link people with systems that provide them with resources, services, and opportunities.

This view of generalist practice grows out of a **holistic view of human behavior.** The emphasis is on the person-in-environment, called by Germain and Gitterman (1980, chap. 1) an "ecological perspective." Perlman (1957, p. 7) uses a somewhat different image to convey the same idea. She talks about it as a "physical-psychological-social past-present-future configuration that [those seeking help] bring to every life-situation [they] encounter" (this is also sometimes referred to as seeing people as a biopsychosocial whole). These views describe human life as a totality in which biological, psychological, cultural, and social structural elements are in constant interaction. It is this complex whole that has to be understood in order to find the resources that will make possible the changes that are needed and desired. This view begins to define the knowledge needed so that the complex web of human life is understandable, an issue addressed in detail in the next chapter. Figure 1.1, adapted from the work of Dee Thornberry, summarizes the points made so far.

Baer and Federico (1978, pp. 86-89) then go on to identify the **competencies** that the generalist social worker needs in order to practice within a holistic perspective. They are the following:

1. Identify and assess situations where relationships between people and social institutions need to be initiated, enhanced, restored, protected, or terminated.
2. Develop and implement a plan for improving the well-being of people based on problem assessment and the exploration of goals and available options.
3. Enhance the problem-solving, coping, and developmental capacities of people.

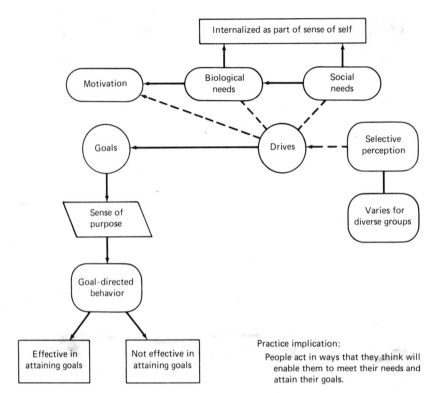

FIGURE 1.1—The Goal-Directed Quality of Human Behavior

4. Link people with systems that provide them with resources, services, and opportunities.
5. Intervene effectively on behalf of populations most vulnerable and discriminated against.
6. Promote the effective and humane operation of the systems that provide people with services, resources, and opportunities.
7. Actively participate with others in creating new, modified, or improved service, resource, and opportunity systems that are more equitable, just, and responsible to consumers of services, and work with others to eliminate those systems that are unjust.
8. Evaluate the extent to which the objectives of the intervention plan were achieved.

9. Continually evaluate one's own professional growth and development through assessment of practice behaviors and skills.
10. Contribute to the improvement of service delivery by adding to the knowledge base of the profession as appropriate and by supporting and upholding the standards and ethics of the profession.

These competencies enable the social work practitioner to achieve the purposes of the profession discussed previously. They reflect a dual focus on people and the environments that either facilitate or obstruct their efforts to plan and attain satisfying lives. Not every helping profession has formulated an explicitly stated set of competencies like the one Baer and Federico developed for social work. However, every profession has developed definitions of what its members ought to do and how they ought to do it, and this is what underlies its view of competent practice. If you remember the simple point that helping in any profession is built around that profession's conception of effective practice, you will not be confused by professional behavior expressed in terms of competencies. Competencies are simply a way of stating very explicitly what a helping profession believes to be essential for effective (competent) practice.

Each competency involves the performance of many specific **helping activities.** For example, competency 3—increasing the coping, problem-solving, and developmental capacities of people—might include providing information to people, giving them emotional support, guiding their efforts to solve problems, linking them with self-help groups, intervening on their behalf in systems that are generating stress that is blocking their developmental efforts, and so on. Competency 6—promoting the effective and humane operation of systems—might involve activities such as writing memos, participating in voter registration efforts, collecting data about the inhumane operation of systems, organizing people within a system so that they can affect its functioning, and so forth.

The competencies, then, identify categories of activities that generalist social workers are expected to master. The specific activities that comprise each competency are many, and will be used at different times and in different ways depending on the specifics of each practice situation. In one situation the person seeking help may need a great deal of information in order to function more effectively. In another case the person may have the necessary information, but may need to be linked with others so that they can collectively use the information most effectively. Table 1.1 summarizes the progression from professional purpose to professional action.

TABLE 1.1—THE FLOW FROM PROFESSIONAL PURPOSE TO PROFESSIONAL ACTION

General framework	Social work as an example
General goal of all helping professions	Help people to function more effectively
Specific purpose of particular helping professions (social work, medicine, nursing, corrections, teaching, and so on)	Develop problem-solving, coping, and developmental capacities of people Link people with resources Promote effective and humane operation of helping systems
Formulation of statements identifying categories of activities members of a particular profession should practice	Ten competencies—for example, making special efforts on behalf of vulnerable and discriminated-against populations
Specific day-to-day practice activities of members of a profession that are derived from the categories of activities (competencies)	Advocating for vulnerable and discriminated-against people, being able to communicate with people from diverse groups, knowing resources available to members of diverse groups, and so on.

THE GENERALIST AS PROBLEM SOLVER

The many activities that generalist helpers perform do not get selected at random. Professional helping makes use of an orderly process for understanding problematic situations, deciding on a course of action, and then carrying it out. This is generally called the **problem-solving process**, and it has six major components:

1. *Communicating with others.* Interaction between people occurs through communication, either verbally, in writing, or visually through body language (facial expressions, posture, style of dress, use of eyes, and so on).
2. *Relating to others.* Through communication a helping relationship is developed. The relationship establishes the mutual trust that enables people to share feelings and information, and to agree to work together to find solutions to problematic situations.
3. *Assessing situations holistically.* Communicating and relating effectively to generate information usable in understanding the major elements of the problematic situation. This understanding allows the helping professional to identify the resources and obstacles that will need to be addressed in the helping effort.
4. *Planning with others.* Once the situation has been clarified, the helper and the person or people seeking help work together to develop plans. All parties agree on both desired outcomes and the activities that will be performed in order to attain them.
5. *Carrying out plans.* After the plan has been negotiated, everyone involved does his/her/their part. For helping people, activities can include providing information, linking people with resources, advocating on behalf of others, providing emotional support, mobilizing resources, helping people to organize on their own behalf, testifying in support of needed social legislation, and so forth.
6. *Evaluating results of helping efforts.* As helping activities proceed, they are monitored to make sure they are having the desired results. If not, plans may be modified.

The problem-solving process will be discussed in more detail in the last chapter. For now, you might want to keep in mind that the six parts do not necessarily occur in sequence. For example, a relationship emerges from early communication, and it deepens and expands as long as communication continues. Assessment continues even after plans have been formulated, because new information may emerge at any time. And evaluation occurs throughout the helping effort, although it may be the focus only at specific points in the helping process.

At this juncture, two points deserve special emphasis. The first is that the purpose of helping guides helping activities. Competencies are developed and helping activities used in order to achieve the purposes of generalist practice—to help people to function more effectively and attain their life goals with maximum access to needed resources and with minimum pain. The problem-solving process is simply a strategy for organizing the specific activities that make up the competencies, as described previously.

The second point is reemphasizing the link between helping activities and knowledge. Remember that in this book we are going to be focusing on knowledge as a base for practice. What we have done so far is provide an overview of the flow from purpose to activity in the helping effort. In the chapters to follow, we will see how all points in this flow have to be grounded in knowledge. Here we can gain an appreciation of this point with a few examples. Let's start with knowledge, as it has an impact on purpose. If we believe (an expression of a value) that mental illness is caused by the devil, then treatment (other than prayer) might not seem appropriate. However, if we know (based on knowledge) that mental illness often has physiological causes, and that social environments can affect it as well, then we are more likely to try to accept some social responsbility for helping people who are mentally ill. Identifying competencies also depends on knowledge. For example, the ten competencies discussed previously resulted from a three-year national study (Baer & Federico, 1978, 1979).

Knowledge is equally important for clarifying day-to-day practice activities. Let us look at communication as an example. Communication involves a complex interactive process of coding information, sending it to others, and having them decode and respond to it. Static interferes with this process, making either the coding, transmission, or decoding process problematic in some way. This knowledge has resulted from thousands of studies of the communication process. As a result of all this information, we know how to improve verbal communication by changing the way a speaker uses the tongue, by attending to perceptual blockages, and by controlling the social environment in which communication occurs. The same basic link between knowledge and practice activities exists in all the other parts of the problem-solving process.

THE SPECIAL IMPORTANCE OF ASSESSMENT

Perhaps the best way to see the impact of knowledge on practice is through assessment. As noted previously, **assessment** is the process of gathering as much information as possible about the practice situation at hand. It is this information that will generate ideas about what the causes of the problematic situation might be, and where the remedies could be found. Let's look at causes first. If a child is being abused by its parents, it could be because its birth was unintended and the child is resented. It could also be because the child is handicapped and the parents are ashamed of it. Alternatively, the marital relationship might be disintegrating with the result that the child is being used as a scapegoat. Each of these possibilities requires knowledge of different kinds of human dynamics—some biological, some psychological, some social-structural, some cultural. Only by patiently gathering as much information as possible can the meaningful causes be identified.

Accuracy is critical because the treatment plan that is developed will reflect the suspectd causes. If the child is resented because its birth was not planned, then counseling, foster care, or even adoption might be appropriate. If the child is handicapped, then medical intervention or some relief to the parents through the provision of home health aides is possible. There is a direct relationship between perceived cause and services selected. Knowledge of the full richness of human behavior is basic to an accurate understanding of causes.

Once the causes have been assessed, appropriate intervention plans (that is, helping plans) must be considered. What do we know about communicating with a resentful parent, or with an abused child who may be too young or too frightened to talk? What sorts of psychological issues can be anticipated with an abused child, regardless of the reasons for the abuse? In child-abuse situations, how much help is needed by the abusing parents, and what obstacles might be encountered in trying to engage such people in helping activities? These, too, are assessment issues. Of course, they cannot be addressed without knowledge of helping activities and skills.

Assessment, then, makes clear why knowledge is so important in professional helping. It helps us to understand the nature of the situation, as well as the options available to deal with it. The next two chapters will emphasize knowledge itself—the specific knowledge needed to understand behavior and practice situations. The following three chapters will move more toward how knowledge is used to make decisions about what practice activities are likely to be most useful in particular situations.

SUMMARY

This chapter has emphasized the close tie between knowledge and the skills of generalist professional helping people. Without knowledge, the effectiveness of helping efforts would be greatly reduced. No matter how much one wants to help, the fullest development of helping skills grows out of knowledge about the goals people have for themselves, acceptable ways of attaining these goals, factors that influence people's behavior in problematic situations, and the helping process. The generalist approach to helping emphasizes the person-in-situation; it takes a holistic view of human behavior. Effective helping occurs only when the many dimensions of problematic situations are addressed, a perspective that results from the helping person having mastered a wide range of biological, behavioral, and social science knowledge. This range of knowledge will be the focus of the next chapter.

STUDY QUESTIONS

1. To what degree do you use a person-in-situation perspective in your daily life? Do you expect people to make allowances for

you under certain circumstances—perhaps because you have less money than some of your friends and cannot afford to go out so often, or because you are smaller than they are and you expect them not to take advantage of you in spite of their larger size? Do you find yourself making allowances for others? Is it ever a problem for you, because you expect something from another person and do not want to have to be concerned with why it may be difficult for that person to do what you think s/he ought to?

2. To what degree do you use a problem-solving approach in your daily life? When you have to make a decision, how do you do so? Have you ever sought help to make a decision? What did the person who helped you do that assisted you? Did you learn anything from that?

3. You have probably taken a course in sociology or psychology or biology; perhaps you have even taken a course in social science research methods. In any of these courses, you would have talked about the scientific method. Compare it to the problem-solving process as summarized in this chapter. Do you see similarities and/or differences?

4. Take any one of the 10 competencies discussed in this chapter. Try to list as many specific activities as you can for that competency. For example, competency 4—linking people with needed resources—could include such activities as giving people pamphlets explaining resources available to them, making telephone calls to see if resources are available, helping someone read a pamphlet, following up to see if someone obtained a resource that was being sought, and so on. Be sure to keep your activities as specific as possible. For example, rather than listing "contacting other agencies to see if resources are available," describe how contacts could actually be made—telephoning, sending a letter, speaking to a colleague about services available, and so forth.

5. Read Exhibit 1.1 at the end of this chapter. Then try to identify the kind of knowledge needed to adequately understand Veronica from a person-in-situation perspective. Go on to explore the knowledge needed to intervene in Veronica's situation. Was anyone in this case functioning as a generalist?

KEY TERMS

Assessment   The process of gathering as much information as possible about the practice situation at hand.

Competency   The ability to perform a function skillfully and effectively.

Generalist   A professional helper who addresses the needs of the whole person, and tries to find the package of resources that will address the range of needs that people have.

Generalist social work practice   Focusing on the interactions between people and the institutions of society that affect the ability of people to accomplish life tasks, realize aspirations and values, and alleviate distress.

Helping activities   Specific behaviors performed by professional helpers which make the competencies operational on a day-to-day basis.

Holistic view of human behavior   A person-in-situation view that sees human behavior as the result of complex interactions between biological, psychological, social-structural, and cultural factors.

Problem-solving process   The orderly process used by professional helpers to understand problematic situations, as well as to formulate and execute plans to address them. Included are communicating with others, relating to others, assessing situations holistically, planning with others, carrying out plans, and evaluating results of helping efforts.

Specialist   A professional helper who provides specific kinds of helping services in particular types of situations.

The following account of the life and death of a 12-year-old prostitute illustrates how important knowledge is for practice. None of the professional helpers who came in contact with Veronica had full information about her as a person-in-situation. It was impossible to extricate her from the web of problems she faced at home, at school, on the streets, and in her own self-identity, because no one was paying attention to the way in which these factors were interacting to keep her in danger. Because knowledge about the causes of her difficulties was incomplete, decisions about how to try to help were also incomplete and thus ineffective. In addition, knowledge was lacking or poorly used, because no one seemed to communicate and relate to her effectively, or to involve her (or her family) in developing meaningful plans to solve her problems. Veronica's tragedy provides an excellent lesson about how important knowledge is for effective helping.

1.1: VERONICA

The first time Veronica Brunson was arrested she was 11 years old. The charge was prostitution. Before another year passed, the police, unaware of her real age, arrested her 11 more times for prostitution.

At the age of 12 Veronica was dead—killed in a mysterious plunge last July from the 10th floor of a shabby midtown hotel frequented by pimps.

Veronica's death, which is being investigated as a possible murder, is one grim crime statistic to the police. But Veronica's life, and her encounters with the city's social service and criminal justice systems in the last year, illustrate the problems and dangers confronting thousands of runaway girls and boys who turn to prostitution to survive alone on the streets of New York.

Six public and private agencies were partly aware of Veronica's difficulties and were supposedly providing aid. But none of the agencies knew her entire history and none intervened quickly enough to rescue her.

"The Brunson case is a classic example of how a kid can float through the entire system without getting any help," said Officer Warren McGinniss of the Police Department's Youth Aid Division, a specialist in runaways. "Even a baby-faced obvious child who claims she is 18 can parade through the entire process—arrest, fingerprinting, arraignment—without anyone asking any questions."

continued

The six agencies—the Department of Social Services, the Board of Education, the Probation Department, the Corporation Counsel's Office, the police, and the Brooklyn Center for Psychotherapy—now cite bureaucratic barriers and communication breakdowns for their failure to act more effectively.

'You can't tell me appropriate intervention couldn't have saved her life," said the Rev. Bruce Ritter, director of Covenant House, a program assisting runaways. "The juvenile-justice and child-welfare systems in the city are chaotic. Programs just don't exist and everyone knows it."

Prostitution by 13-, 14- and 15-year-olds posing as older persons is no longer rare, but arrest for prostitution at the age of 11 is believed by vice squad detectives to be the youngest recorded here in decades.

In the summer of 1976, Veronica Brunson was 11, living in a fatherless home with her mother, Emma, who is now 34, and her brothers, Carson, 17, Douglas, 18, and Willie, 19.

Mrs. Brunson, unable to find work in her home state of North Carolina, had moved to Brooklyn when Veronica was 2. The family lived in a neatly kept, three-bedroom apartment in the Housing Authority's Marlboro Houses in Bensonhurst. In addition to their rent, the family received $318 monthly from welfare.

No Sign of Delinquency

By 1976 each of the Brunson boys had been arrested several times and had been in the juvenile courts. In contrast, Veronica, her mother, teachers and friends agreed, was well behaved, with no sign of delinquency. . . .

Pinched for money, Mrs. Brunson said she had made most of Veronica's clothing herself. "I tried to give her everything a little girl could want—clothing, food and some pocket money," Mrs. Brunson said in an interview. "She was a good little girl and if I told her to be home by six, she always was."

The Trouble Begins

At school, Veronica was a poor student. She had been left back once in the elementary grades, and in 1975 she was transferred to a special program for slow learners at Public School 253 in the Brighton Beach section. Her first year in the program went reasonably well, according to her teachers, and she was promoted to the sixth grade in June 1976.

Veronica's runaway problem suddenly began in midsummer of 1976, Mrs. Brunson said.

"One evening she came home with an older girl whose name was Diana who she met at Coney Island," Mrs. Brunson recalled. "Diana said she was 18 and wanted Veronica to spend a few days with her over the bridge (in Manhattan). I said no

continued

because I didn't think that girl Diana would be a good influence."

Several days later, Mrs. Brunson continued, Veronica disappeared for the first time, staying away from home for three days. On her return, Veronica told her mother she had stayed with her new friend Diana in Manhattan.

That July, Veronica continued to leave home for two- or three-day periods. Mrs. Brunson said that she had failed to report her daughter to the police as a missing person because Veronica would occasionally telephone her.

When the new school year began in September of 1976, Veronica failed to appear at P.S. 253. Checking into Veronica's absence, Bernard Lew, her guidance counselor, said he was told by her mother that she had been missing for more than a month. Mr. Lew said he urged Mrs. Brunson to contact the police.

First Arrested Last Fall

Police records show that Veronica was reported missing for the first time on September 19, 1976, after the school term had begun, and that her family said she had been missing for six weeks.

One day after the missing person report was filed, Veronica was arrested on a prostitution charge. A plainclothes officer said she had solicited him on West 42nd Street. The 11-year-old gave the police her real age and identity, and she was released in Mrs. Brunson's custody, pending action by the Family Court, which hears all criminal matters involving children up to the age of 16.

When Veronica returned to P.S. 253 in the autumn of 1976 her teachers and counselors were unaware of the arrest. Nevertheless, all of them said they noticed significant changes in her.

The year before she had dressed inconspicuously, almost shabbily. Now she used facial makeup and wore expensive looking, color-coordinated clothing, jewelry, high-heeled shoes and nylon stockings. . . .

The teachers, who were ignorant of her arrest, were most concerned about her chronic absenteeism, which eventually reached 121 of 180 school days that year.

Mr. Lew said that numerous telephone inquiries by staff members had been made about Veronica's absenses. Her mother or brothers usually replied that the girl was ill, the teachers said.

Case Kept Out of Court

In the aftermath of the first arrest, Veronica and her mother were interviewed on October 8 by a Manhattan Family Court probation department officer. At that time, the officer decided that the matter should be kept out of

continued

19

the court, where Veronica could have been declared a "person in need of supervision," and possibly taken from her mother.

Instead, the probation officer, after consulting with child-welfare officials in the Social Services Department, decided that the case could be "adjusted" by sending Veronica for outpatient counseling at the Brooklyn Center for Psychotherapy, a private institution.

Under a policy of "diversion," the Probation Department tries to help youngsters without exposing them to formal court hearings before a judge.

Last autumn, the department, having made no inquiries at Veronica's school, had no inkling of her increasing truancy, her unorthodox dress or conversations with teachers about being recruited by pimps. Satisfied that the girl was getting adequate attention from the Social Services Department and the private psychotherapy center, the department closed her case in December. . . .

"She Was Still a Child"

Mr. Knepper said that Veronica had made one of her infrequent visits to his classroom on her 12th birthday, December 5, because she knew he was planning a party for her.

"She wanted that kind of attention and affection," the teacher said. "Despite all of her supposed sophistication it was obvious that she was still a child

who wanted someone to help her." . . .

With Veronica no longer attending school, Mrs. Brunson and her son, Douglas, said that they were unable to prevent her running from home for brief periods. Mrs. Brunson acknowledged that she "sometimes" failed to report her daughter missing because she was confident of ultimately persuading her to return home and to school.

By May, Veronica was a familiar figure on the "Minnesota strip," a seedy part of Eighth Avenue from 40th to 50th Streets that is favored by street walkers. On the strip, Veronica, now five-feet, two-inches tall and weighing 110 pounds was known to other prostitutes as "Shortie" and by her childhood nickname, "Bay-Bay."

Police and court records show that between May 7 and July 18 Veronica was arrested 11 times in the midtown area. Usually she was charged with loitering for the purpose of prostitution, the most common misdemeanor used by the police to harass and temporarily remove prostitutes from the streets.

Used Fictitous Names

Either through coaching from a pimp or older prostitutes, Veronica carried no identification and gave the police a fictitious name and address and said she was 18 when arrested. Two of

continued

her aliases were Vanessa Brown and Paula Brunson.

She always pleaded guilty in Criminal Court and often was released after being held overnight at a police station. But for two convictions she was sentenced to a total of 12 days, which she served among adult prisoners in the Women's House of Detention.

Only once during this series of arrests did Veronica reveal her real identity and age. Police Officer David Olenchalk, who arrested Veronica on May 12 on Eighth Avenue and 46th Street, said she wore a shoulder-length black wig and "easily passed for 18 or 19." While being booked at the Midtown North stationhouse, Veronica abruptly acknowledged her age and asked the police to call her mother.

Released in the custody of her mother, Veronica was referred for a second time to the Family Court. At an interview with a Probation Department Officer on May 20, Veronica disclosed that she had been arrested several times and had been in jail on Rikers Island.

Gerald Hecht, the city's Probation Director, said department files indicated that at the May 20 meeting, Mrs. Brunson "exhibited ambivalence about placement" of Veronica in an institution or a foster home and another interview was scheduled for a month later.

Crucial Postponement

Several hours after the May 20 interview, Veronica, once more using an alias, was arrested on a prostitution charge.

Dr. Judianne Densen-Gerber, a psychiatrist who is president of the Odyssey Institute, a group of private centers for emotionally disturbed children, said that the month-long postponement by the Probation Department may have been crucial for Veronica.

"By admitting she was 12 years old, the child was clearly saying 'Help me, do something for me now.' " Dr. Densen-Gerber asserted. "Time is a critical factor for these children. They can't tolerate delay. It's like telling a person who's just had a heart attack to come back to the hospital in a month or two."

Veronica failed to appear for her scheduled interview at the Probation Department on June 29. Yet none of the three agencies—Probation, the Corporation Counsel or the Social Services Department—would petition the Family Court to have her picked up as a "person in need of supervision" . . .

With the Family Court proceedings in legal limbo, Veronica remained on the "Minnesota strip," occasionally getting arrested. Her last known arrest occurred on July 18 when she gave her age as 18. Pleading in

continued

Criminal Court to a charge of prostitution, she jumped bail rather than serve a 15-day sentence. . . .

"There are two stories on the street about her death," said Lieut. James Gallagher, the commander of the prostitution squad in Manhattan South area. "One that she was thrown out by a pimp and the other that she was having a fight with her pimp and fell out the window while sitting on the ledge."

"It's not unbelievable that a pimp would throw a girl out a window," he continued. "They brutalize girls if they hold back money, get fresh or try to get away from them."

Even in death, Veronica remained forgotten. It took the police nine days to identify her. Her fingerprints, taken in her "adult" arrests, linked her to fictitious names and addresses. Since no fingerprints are taken of children under the age of 16 there was no way of identifying her through Family Court records.

Neither Veronica's family nor any of the agencies reported her missing even after she failed to appear in Family Court. Detectives traced her after learning from Times Square prostitutes that she came from a Brooklyn Housing project and that her family name might be Brunson. . . .

REFERENCES

Baer, B., & Federico, R. (1978). *Educating the baccalaureate social worker,* Vol. I. Cambridge, MA: Ballinger Publishing Co.

Baer, B., & Federico, R. (1979). *Educating the baccalaureate social worker,* Vol II. Cambridge, MA: Ballinger Publishing Co.

Berelson, B., & Steiner, G. (1964). *Human behavior: An inventory of scientific findings.* New York: Harcourt, Brace and World.

Federico, R. (1984). *The social welfare institution: An introduction.* Lexington, MA: D. C. Heath.

Germain, C., & Gitterman, A. (1980). *The life model of social work practice.* New York: Columbia University Press.

Kahn, A., & Kamerman, S. (1976). *Social services in international perspective.* Washington, D.C.: U. S. Government Printing Office.

Konle, Carolyn (1982). *Social work day-to-day.* New York: Longman Inc.

Perlman, H. H. (1957). *Social casework.* Chicago: University of Chicago Press.

Smalley, R. (1967). *Theory for social work practice.* New York: Columbia University Press.

Zimbalist, S. (1977). *Historic themes and landmarks in social welfare research.* New York: Harper & Row.

2

THE DIMENSIONS OF HUMAN BEHAVIOR

CHAPTER OVERVIEW

Human behavior is enormously complex and diverse, in part because of the multiple sources—biological, psychological, cultural, social structural—from which it springs. Chapter 1 discussed the necessity of the helping effort being rooted in knowledge and commitment, and presented the generalist-specialist continuum as a way of organizing knowledge for the purpose of intervention. This chapter will present a framework that is helpful both in identifying specific concepts that are useful to the social welfare professional and in integrating them into a pattern that sees life as a complex but comprehensive whole.

Pulling together information from diverse sources into a perspective that is useful in designing action plans based on rational decision making is indeed an awesome task. While the existing body of knowledge in the biological, behavioral, and social sciences at times appears frightfully incomplete and inconsistent, the professional is nonetheless called upon to intervene in the lives of individuals, groups, organizations, communities, and societies to effect change. Waiting until all the facts are in could easily mean "fiddling while Rome burns." The urgency of the professional task frequently requires immediate action, and decisions must be made based on available information. Alan Mendelsohn (1980, p. 80) speaks to this issue:

> The realities of working with people in the vast social landscape serve only to identify the lack of knowledge of human beings and their environment and force the social worker to the painful acknowledgement that all the answers are not yet known.

The framework presented in this chapter focuses on the dimensions of human behavior and the knowledge base that needs to be mastered, integrated, and applied by the generalist practitioner for effective helping. A brief overview of foundation content from "core" academic disciplines (the biological, social, and behavioral sciences) will be followed by an analysis of the various dimensions of human behavior that inform generalist practice. Exhibits at the end of the chapter are offered to further illustrate the multiple sources from which human behavior springs, and to serve as a stimulus for further discussion.

MASTERY, INTEGRATION, AND APPLICATION

Knowledge about human behavior includes both explanatory and intervention knowledge. The academic disciplines, in addressing the dimensions of human behavior, have as one of their primary purposes the acquisition of knowledge for the sake of understanding the human condition. This is **explanatory knowledge**; it seeks to explain behavior rather than alter it. Other possible goals may be the prediction and control of behavior. For such action-oriented purposes, **intervention knowledge** is needed. The methods used to gain either type of knowledge are as varied as the disciplines represented. The scientific method is one pathway followed in collecting data. This is the method with which most social welfare professionals are familiar. Other avenues equally useful for explaining (or at least illuminating) the many-faceted sources of human behavior are the arts and the humanities.

Explanatory knowledge guides the professional in answering "why" questions, and calls upon him/her to utilize principles and concepts from anthropology, biology, economics, political science, psychology, and sociology. Intervention knowledge, useful in addressing "how" and "what" questions, calls for an integration of explanatory knowledge and prior experience in using knowledge to achieve change. The human service professional, then, is given the societal mandate not only to understand the human condition, but to influence and change it.

Explanatory and intervention knowledge are not mutually exclusive categories; their separation is only useful for clarity of presentation. In reality, issues arising from practice situations (intervention) often become the questions upon which future research (explanatory) builds. The relationship between knowledge and practice is a reciprocal one in that the application of existing knowledge in practice often yields a measure of its accuracy. Existing knowledge, then, directs and informs intervention and helps assess why such efforts were helpful or not; in turn, practice identifies gaps and weaknesses in our existing knowledge base.

Knowledge shapes and focuses the helping professional's understanding of human behavior and the social environment in three interrelated and cumulative ways:

1. Familiarity with biological, social, and behavioral science concepts helps to explain the multifaceted dimensions of individual, group, and social-structural behavior. These basic concepts come from human biology, anthropology, economics, political science, psychology, and sociology.
2. Integration of concepts from the above multiple sources, and identification of those with particular utility for practice, help develop a holistic view of human behavior.
3. Application of integrated knowledge to concrete situations as part of one's practice guides intervention efforts.

The interrelated and cumulative tasks of mastery, integration, and application give form and substance to the professional's understanding of the dimensions of human behavior. They become the steps through which knowledge about the biological, psychological, cultural, and social-structural bases of behavior directs practice activities.

The following example will illustrate what is meant by the cumulative and interrelated manner in which the professional uses knowledge.

> John, a 49-year-old, white male, first came to the Neighborhood Health Clinic with complaints of difficulty in concentration, poor appetite, frequent swings in moods, increasing irritability noted both at work and at home, and a general feeling of lethargy and depression. Following an especially volatile outbreak of anger at work, his supervisor recommended he have a complete medical examination. John tried to convince himself there was no reason for serious concern, and it was only after several weeks of constant prodding that he finally agreed to set up an appointment for a physical examination. As part of the clinic's application procedure each applicant must first be interviewed by the intake worker.

This vignette points to the importance of the intake worker (a generalist) being knowledgeable about the interrelated aspects of John's situation in order to be sensitive to these areas as they come up in the interview. The biological (expressed here in terms of his physical symptomology), psychological (his use of the defense mechanism of denial), cultural (beliefs about the uses of medicine and/or the meaning of illness), and social-structural (the impact of illness on dynamics of the family, the fear of its possible effect on continued employability) are so interrelated that their separation is at best artificial, and at worst impedes progress. Pinpointing what is cause and what is effect may well be beyond the purview of the generalist intake worker, so the services of several specialists (doctors, nutritionists, X-ray technicians) may be called upon to complete the assessment package. Nonetheless, the generalist practitioner needs to have some way of organizing the vast amount of information available about human behavior into its component parts, and then a way of seeing the components in terms of their relationship to each other.

What follows is a breakdown of the primary sources (dimensions) of human behavior and then a review of selected concepts useful to the generalist practitioner. These dimensions and concepts provide a helpful base for organizing and using knowledge for intervention purposes.

FOUR SOURCES OF BEHAVIOR

The four principle sources of human behavior are biological, psychological, social-structural, and cultural. Part of human behavior is biologically determined, deriving from the genetic inheritance that establishes potentials and limits for a person's behavior. The current literature of both the social and the biological sciences is replete with arguments as to the relative influence of genetics on behavior. Indeed, sociobiologists contend that all social behavior can be explained genetically. An infant will automatically grasp and move its limbs because of species reflexes (genetically programmed predispositions). The sucking reflex, however, may not be present in an infant who has a genetic disorder that causes brain damage. In some cases such innate deficits can be compensated for through learning, whereas in others the potential for remedy may be limited. Potentials for behavior are biologically created, but in humans certain social conditions are usually needed for them to be realized. While a brain-damaged child may be unable to move its limbs because of an organic deficit, a child who is not brain damaged may move its limbs only rarely because it lacks stimulation from others. Although the behavioral result is similar in both cases, the cause is biological in one and social in the other. This underlines the importance of the interaction of biological and social-structural forces. The research of sociobiologists explores the extent to which even such social behaviors as altruism, aggression, and adherence to group loyalty serve to enhance species survival (Barash, 1977).

Biological potential is influenced by the cultural context in which it occurs, as well as by psychological and social-structural variables. Awareness of the interrelationship of these variables is translated into practice in infant stimulation programs, maternal and child care programs, and various nutritional programs for pregnant women and young children. Such programs recognize that the realization of genetic potential is influenced by such nonbiological factors as the psychological well-being of the caretaker and the social conditions that affect whether needed environmental resources are available. Technological sophistication brought about by computerization has also affected biological functioning by making possible the early identification of genetically at-risk populations. Emerging roles for helping professionals in areas such as genetic counseling further evidences how technology has begun to control what in the not-so-distant past was seen as biologically predetermined.

Midlife serves as another point on the biological continuum from birth to death when one finds dramatic evidence of cultural and social-structural variables influencing biological events. Knowledge about metabolic changes accompanying midlife may be explored in the biological science component of the curriculum. Such changes may include changes in hormonal secretions, changes in various organ systems, or degenerative changes that increase one's vulnerability to illness and organ dysfunction. Significance is added when the psychosocial aspects of midlife are examined. The doubts and conflicts often accompanying those physical changes (biological dimension of behavior) take form in highly personal ways. As a result, they require an understanding of the life experiences of each individual (psychological dimension of behavior). Social-structural and cultural dimensions are added when one examines the belief systems cultures perpetuate about midlife, and the resources or obstacles encountered as one progresses through this life stage.

A second source of behavior is psychological, resulting from a person's perceptual, cognitive, and emotional development.

Humans are unique in that the amount of the behavior controlled by reflexes is limited. Most (but not all) of what we can do we have learned through the use of biological/psychological potential. Human behavior is operationalized through the development of perceptual, cognitive, and motor capacities, as well as through the development of personality structures that mediate between individual needs and the social-structural environment. The development of psychological components is heavily dependent on human interaction—the process of individuals relating to each other in supportive, competitive, or even destructive ways. Once psychological capacities are developed they become important determinants of both individual and collective behavior. Human aging serves as yet another example of how psychological, cultural, and social-structural factors have an impact on the biological dimension of behavior. The issue of longevity, for instance, illustrates how biological potentials may be realized to their fullest extent only in a supportive environment. While the puzzle of aging is not yet answered by any of several biological theories advanced, Kimmel (1980) points out that both hereditary and external factors (marital status, disease, environment) are specifically related to longevity. Self-perception and self-concepts become the psychological corrolaries of the biological and social structural sources of behavior.

Psychological growth and development, like biological, do not exist in a vacuum, but are responsive to the cultural and social-structural context in which they occur. Developing a positive self-image, for example, is supported by an environment that applauds one's efforts and provides the resources (interpersonal and financial) to accelerate the accomplishment of one's goals. The social-structural climate, however, could just as easily present obstacles to building a positive self-concept. Ageism, racism, sexism, and homophobia (fear of homosexuality) are examples of some of the powerful ways the cultural matrix has an impact on one's sense of self-worth. Some elderly people, for example, have a seriously damaged self-concept as a result of having internalized society's negative stereotypes about old age. Societal supports have crumbled and a series of losses have ensued—income, physical functioning capacity, social roles. Some programs attempt to at least partially reverse this downhill spiral. The Administration on Aging, through its congregate meal program (a social-structural arrangement that is part of the Older Americans Act), acknowledges the interrelationship between the need for programs that meet nutritional (biological) needs as well as providing opportunities for socializing with others (psychological). This service attempts to reduce both nutritional deficiency and social isolation, thereby recognizing how closely intertwined these sources of behavior are.

Existing programs need to increase their efforts to combat the cultural baggage that perpetuates ageist stereotypes. These stereotypes are so deeply embedded in our institutional fabric that even becoming aware of them is at times difficult, yet the pervasiveness of the message that young is good, old is bad, is constant. Reversing cultural beliefs and their internalization about a biological fact (age), requires simultaneous action at the cultural, psychological, and sociostructural levels. This point is illustrated by Exhibit 2.2 at the end of the chapter.

Social structures represent a third source of behavior. Social structures, such as the family and the economic system, exist to organize and pattern social interaction. This structuring is important for social order, making it possible for people to behave with some degree of predictability. Once structures exist, they control behavior and exert pressures to maintain themselves. These pressures then have to be balanced with the individual needs that these structures are meant to serve. Indeed, the issue of balancing individual and societal needs is ever-present in human life and is inevitable given the fact that humans depend primarily on social interaction rather than on genetically programmed behavior. Thus social structures serve to motivate behavior as well as to organize and control it.

Students often have a much more difficult time understanding the impact of sociostructural variables on human behavior than they do with biological and psychological ones. This is partly due to the abstract nature of the material. It is impossible to "touch" an institution, for instance. But the difficulty also stems from the persistent cultural belief that the individual can overcome environmental deficiencies through the development of a strong character. Explicating the impact of social-structural arrangements on biological and psychological development becomes one of the goals of studying human behavior and the social environment. Sociostructural determinants of behavior demand focusing not only the family and the economic institutions as mentioned above, but also the programs, policies, and services that employ and pay us, and the political structures that govern and control us. Where one fits in the stratification system colors a whole host of factors, including such different things as the frequency with which we have sex and the positions we prefer while engaging in sexual activity.

Many of the social problems plaguing American society are rooted in social-structural arrangements that benefit some groups at the expense of others. Gans (1971) points out how poverty serves the needs of the non-poor, for instance, in that it creates employment for social workers, provides workers who will work for low pay at undesirable jobs, gives the leisure classes a tax-deductible charitable contribution, and maintains a pool of people to populate slum housing. Addressing the problems of poverty, according to Gans' analysis, necessitates major institutional change, including shifting the power between the poor and the non-poor. The idea of changing individuals is easier for most of us to entertain than the idea of changing society. The tendency for outmoded social structures to perpetuate themselves speaks to their resiliency.

Finally, all human behavior occurs within a cultural context. Culture embodies the values, knowledge, and material technology that people learn to accept as appropriate and desirable. Therefore culture establishes the parameters that guide and often limit people's thinking and behavior. Culture represents humankind's master plan—it molds our way of explaining the world and charts the limits of allowable behavior. Its influence on human action takes on added significance in a society composed of many cultural groups. The United States' society, for example, is composed of a diverse range of ethnic, socioeconomic, and life-style groups, each of which influences the thinking and behavior of its members. Because one person may belong to several cultural groups simultaneously—Roman Catholic, single parent, Italian-American, woman with few economic resources—each cultural influence on behavior may be subtle and diverse. These influences become even more complex given the need to create a viable culture that integrates many disparate groups. As with socioeconomic influences on behavior, cultural influences are seldom directly observable, at least to the untrained eye. Their effects, however, are nonetheless powerful and pervasive. The individual is rarely conscious of the role culture plays in determining his/her behavior. Cultural practices become so habitual we often think of them as "natural." For example, we may consider it "natural" for women to shave their legs and armpits, and unnatural for men (except swimmers or dancers, perhaps) to do likewise. Conforming to cultural stereotypes eliminates many of the individual decisions one must make in any given day, and thus conformity accounts for much of the predictability in human behavior. Challenging stereotypes, on the other hand, often results in the imposition of negative sanctions. Culture can be seen as the composite of all humankind's learned behavior, and it guides and instructs human beings in much the same way that instincts guide other animal species. At several levels, then, culture is an important source of behavior.

While it is possible to analyze the four sources of behavior discussed above separately, in reality they work together to shape human life. Each human being has a unique biological endowment that creates his/her behavior potentials. The degree to which this potential is realized, however, is heavily influenced by our culture, our psychological development, and our social-structural environment. For example, a woman who is born with the potential for high intellectual achievement, but lives in a culture that does not value intelligence in women, is unlikely to have many opportunities to develop her intellectual capacities to their fullest potential. If, for instance, her family values intellectual achievement, and has sufficient economic resources, it may take advantage of the educational resources society provides. If, on the other hand, the family's values concur with the culture's devaluation of education for women, or if the family lacks the economic resources necessary to finance an education, the woman will most likely have few opportunities to develop her biological potential. Indeed, in such a situation the woman may even begin to think of herself as unintelligent or deviant if others treat her as such.

Labeling theory explains how individuals, having internalized cultural stereotypes, often behave in ways consistent with social expectations. Schur (1984) uses labeling theory to document the process whereby society devalues women, and he uses women's relative position on the socioeconomic and prestige ladders as objective evidence of their devalued status. Biological potentials are thus thwarted by cultural and social-structural variables. Similar experiences of devaluation were reported by Malcolm X in his autobiography. Always at the top of his class academically, he was nonetheless consistently advised by his teachers that he should abandon his dream to attend law school and choose a life work more in keeping with what they (his teachers) felt appropriate for a black man—a semiskilled trade. These examples illustrate that it is the *interaction* of biological, social-structural, psychological, and cultural sources of behavior, that, generally speaking, has the most significance for determining an individual's life experience. Any one of them viewed in isolation is far less influential than when viewed in interaction with the other sources.

UNDERSTANDING THE FOUR SOURCES OF BEHAVIOR: BASIC CONCEPTS

It is possible to understand each of the four sources of behavior only after one understands the basic concepts that describe and explain specific components of behavior. These concepts are generated and codified in the major social, biological, and behavioral science disciplines, most importantly human biology, psychology, sociology, anthropology, political science, and economics. Many readers will have already studied some or all of these disciplines and have been introduced to their most important concepts. Others will be in the process of doing so. It is important to study concepts in the context of their respective disciplines. This provides the historical and methodological perspectives needed to fully understand them in all their richness.

Throughout this book concepts will be used in various combinations dictated by the need to view helping situations in a holistic way. Again, a social welfare professional needs to understand as many aspects of a situation as possible. As noted previously, this includes the biological, psychological, social-structural, and cultural components of behavior as they interact with each other. Before concepts explaining or describing various aspects of situations can be used in the combinations necessary to understand a particular situation, each must be understood individually. It is this integration of concepts that makes a holistic approach possible in practice. While the following summary of the

concepts will provide a useful common base for the rest of the
book, three cautions should be observed. First, this is only a
summary. There is no substitute for the level of understanding
gained from a study of these concepts in their respective
disciplines. Second, this summary is of a selective nature. The
concepts presented here are only a selection of those that are
potentially useful in professional practice. The reader should be
constantly alert to others which may also be useful. Third, resist
fragmentation of concepts, remember that human life is a
complex whole, and concepts discussed in one area (such as the
biological source of behavior) frequently have applicability in
other areas as well.

In order to avoid a random listing, concepts will be organized
under the familiar headings of biological, psychological, social-
structural, and cultural.[1] Like any organizing framework, this one
is somewhat arbitrary; it has been selected in order to avoid the
separateness that can be generated by disciplinary boundaries. It
also reduces the framework to four parts—a manageable number.
Before beginning, remember that this is only a selection of very
briefly summarized concepts.

Basic Biological Concepts

The most fundamental concept of human behavior is life itself.
The physiological process of life is the management of complex
chemical processes mediated by the brain through an elaborate
series of neurological impulses. The *brain* serves as a command
center that activates (or fails to activate) the chemical substances
and their interactions that begin at conception. At *conception* a
female's egg is fertilized by a male's sperm. This union combines
genetic information from the two parents in the form of 46
chromosomes[2] which then chart the newly conceived individual's

[1]Readers should consult the reference and additional reading lists at the end of
the chapter for titles of works providing further elaboration of the concepts used
here. No attempt is made to specifically cite each one in the text itself, as such an
effort would be unnecessarily tedious and repetitive.

[2]Chromosomes are the carriers of genetic information. They are strands in
the nuclei of somatic and sex cells along which genes are arranged in linear order.
The gene is the basic unit of heredity. See Benjamin Wolman, ed., *Dictionary of
Behavioral Science* (New York: Van Nostrand Reinhold, 1973) pp. 61, 156.

biological potential. Each combination of genetic information is multigenerational as well as unique. It is multigenerational in that the parents carry genetic information from their parents, which may in turn be passed on to the newly conceived generation. This is true even for genetic information that is not physiologically evident in the parent as, for example, when red-haired children are born to parents neither of whom have red hair. Genetic combinations are unique in that a mixing process occurs during fertilization so that only some genetic elements of each parent become part of the newly created fetus. In addition, *mutations* may occur in genes to change them from their original form when they are transmitted at conception. While mutations are relatively rare, they and the natural genetic mixing process that occurs at conception ensure human difference. Thus a person's genetic inheritance becomes an important basis for his/her social uniqueness, because social development depends upon the potentials created by genetic inheritance.

Because of this genetically defined potential for behavior, human beings have tremendous *adaptation* potential. Rather than being guided primarily by *genetically programmed reflexes* that predispose the organism to react in set ways to particular situations, the human being can make use of many types of resources in many different ways. For example, nutritional needs are met by utilizing a variety of plant and animal substances. This flexibility makes it possible for humans to adapt to any number of geographical and climatic environments. This example demonstrates that genetic flexibility in humans is extremely far-reaching. Not only can humans physiologically process many types of nutrients (meat, dairy, vegetables, and so on), they also have the capacity to learn how to process potential nutrients so that they can be better digested (through curing processes, cooking, and storage strategies to avoid spoilage, to name a few). It is the complex interplay of chemical digestive processes, brain development and functioning capacity, and skeletal-muscular potential that makes humans so adaptable. All of these factors are part of the genetic potential that humans as a species inherit, although each individual's particular set of potentials (and limits) is unique. As will be discussed later, part of the human inheritance is the potential for language, which makes culture possible. The interaction of culture and biology then becomes extremely important in human behavior by preserving and transmitting those types of adaptations that have proven most effective.

Once created, life must be actively sustained or it will quickly end. Part of the human's genetic inheritance is a set of instructions that cause physiological growth and development to occur in an orderly process throughout the *life cycle,* the period of life from conception to death. When the genetic plan is able to unfold because the resources needed to permit growth and development have been provided, we can talk about physiological *health.* As noted earlier, the genetic plan can accommodate extensive variation and adaptation while moving the human organism through the stages of increasing size, complexity, and autonomy that characterize growth and development. In a state of health, there is a relatively stable interaction and exchange among the various components of the human body. For example, enough blood is pumped by the heart and adequately oxygenated by the lungs to feed the muscles so that they contract and relax in the process of use that leads to their increase in size and strength. This view of the human body is a *systemic* one, focusing on the way the parts (organs, bones, muscles, blood, nerves, and so on) of a whole (the biological body) work together to allow the whole to maintain itself in its environment. This maintenance of a relatively steady state of a system is called *homeostasis.* Obviously, the concept of systems is a complex one, referring to a hierarchy of wholes of which the body is only one (others would include the family, the community, society, and so on). In chapter 3 systems will be analyzed in more detail.

Because the end of life is part of the life cycle,*degenerative processes* are part of the developmental process. As the human body ages, the genetic plan begins to enact the deterioration of cells at a rate and in a pattern unique to each person. Degenerative processes are strongly affected by stress, which pushes a person toward or beyond his or her adaptive capacity. Stress may occur at any point in the life cycle, and is often experienced in the form of inadequate nutrition (lack of the basic nutrients needed for physiological health), inadequate nurturance (lack of the basic protection and caring needed for psychological well-being, which strongly affects physiological health), and an environment that lacks basic life-sustaining and life-enriching resources. Stress often generates *pain* as a warning that some part of the system is being pushed toward its adaptive limit. There may also be a relationship between degenerative processes and *deficits*. The potential for growth and development may be limited, sometimes severely, by parts of the human system that are deficient or whose functioning is severely constrained. This can be due to genetic inheritance or traumas, such as accidents. Brain damage, for example, is a deficit that may affect the whole neurological structure and the ability of the brain to manage other physiological processes. The existence of major physical deficits often interacts with and accelerates the degenerative processes that are a natural part of the life cycle.

Life ends in *death*, the point at which the human body is no longer able to sustain itself. Death is inevitable and is the result of genetically programmed patterns. Death may also be caused by stress that pushes the body beyond its adaptive limits—the *trauma*, or shock, of blood loss caused by an accident, for example. Although conception and death are fundamentally biological processes, their significance is most often defined by the social context in which they occur. For example, the deaths of an infant, a middle-aged breadwinner, and an elderly person have very different impacts on other individuals and social groups, such as family members and family units. Survivors react differently to the death of someone following a long chronic illness than they would to a sudden accidental death, or to a murder, no matter what the age of the deceased. Religious beliefs and practices associated with funeral rituals demonstrate how cultures deal with death and mourning differently. Before moving now to basic psychological concepts (and then social-structural and cultural

---

TABLE 2.1—A SUMMARY OF
BASIC BIOLOGICAL CONCEPTS

Adaptation	Health
Brain	Homeostasis
Chromosomes	Life
Conception	Life cycle
Death	Mutation
Deficit	Pain
Degenerative processes	Stress
Genetically programmed reflexes	System
	Trauma

---

ones), it is important to recall that human behavior is only understandable as the interplay of biological, psychological, social-structural, and cultural factors. It is also suggested that you review the biological concepts presented in this section. You should be able to briefly define each of the concepts in Table 2.1.

Basic Psychological Concepts

People's responses to their environment are dependent on their understanding of it, which, in turn, is the result of psychological processes combining biological and social factors. In terms of understanding the environment, three biologically based capacities are of particular importance. **Perception** is the ability to see, hear, smell, feel, and touch, and develop organized responses to the sensory characteristics of the environment. The multiple stimuli that fill the natural and social environment require the capacity to perceive selectively to avoid becoming confused and overwhelmed. For example, the residents of large cities can ignore many of the sounds and movements in their environment, focusing instead on their immediate surroundings and objectives. Visitors, on the other hand, frequently experience tension and confusion until they learn how to be more selective. **Cognition** is the ability to process and organize sensory information in order to manipulate the environment to achieve one's own goals. This occurs through learning, memory, and the ability to focus attention in specific situations. **Affect** is the feelings and emotions that become attached to information derived from perceptions and cognitive functioning. All three—perception, cognition, and affect—have physiological roots. The workings of the eye, the functioning of the brain, and hormonal responses to a threatening situation are all examples. However, the social environment is obviously a powerful factor in the ways these biologically based capacities develop and are used, demonstrating again the close interaction of biological and social sources of behavior.

The flexibility with which humans are blessed due to their genetic inheritance adds another dimension to perception, cognition, and affect. The social environments in which people live attribute particular meaning to certain events and objects. These meanings are learned through the process of **socialization,** through which an individual acquires the beliefs, customs, values, and attitudes of his/her culture or social group. Through socialization we learn what we are expected to do and how we are to accomplish it. Socialization is at work when we use our cognitive capacities to learn to do some things and are relatively unconcerned about learning to do others. For example, Europeans consider it valuable to learn several languages because of the close geographical proximity of other countries, but the relative geographical isolation of the United States has tended to make this less of a perceived concern.

Socialization influences our perceptions, which in turn influence the amount and type of affect, or emotional investment we accord to a person, event, or object. People perceived as important evoke feelings of affection or respect. Situations that we have learned are threatening or confusing become associated with feelings of apprehension, fear, or inadequacy. Our behavior is therefore often determined more by our subjective interpretation of events than by their objective reality.

The physiological potentials for perception, cognition, and emotion become part of the individual's response to the environment. **Personality** is the integrating psychological structure that develops to help the individual function in the environment. Personality is composed of fairly consistent patterns of responses to situations, patterns that are consistent within an individual, but differ from one individual to the next. Whereas some people may respond to threatening situations by running away, others respond to them with excitement. Some people express anger very directly, while others find it difficult to let people know when they are angry. In these and countless other ways people differ in their responses to situations according to their personality characteristics.

The personality's task of mediating between the individual and the environment is closely related to the individual's needs. Some needs—for example, for eating and resting—are primarily physical and do not have to be learned. Others are much more social, such as feeling secure, competent, and loved. Needs are most often learned through interaction with others and through the socialization that results. For example, while no one has to be taught to need food, we all do have to learn what foods we need in order to be healthy, the steps we need to take when preparing food, and the need to develop good table manners so as to be accepted in polite company.

Needs, both primary and learned, are powerful *motivations* for behavior. Most people try to maximize experiences they perceive as pleasurable, and having one's needs met is usually seen in this way. People are, therefore, motivated to engage in need-meeting behavior. As noted earlier, identification of needs to be met and appropriate ways of meeting them are often learned through interaction and socialization. Personality develops as an individual learns how to use his/her perceptual and cognitive abilities to meet needs and thus experience pleasurable physical sensations and social approval. In managing the interaction of the person and the environment so that need-meeting can occur, various psychological **defenses** are used. These include projection, repression, sublimation, reaction formation, regression, and others. Defenses help the personality to keep a balance between the desires of the individual and the demands of the environment. They are functional tools for the personality except when they become so rigid and elaborate that they block the individual's ability to accurately perceive physical needs or social reality.

It should be increasingly evident that the boundaries between biological, psychological, sociostructural, and cultural sources of human behavior are very fluid. The biological foundations of behavior are basic to life, but conditions of the physical and social environment are powerful determinants of the developing personality. The personality in turn becomes a very significant factor in perceiving and meeting biological needs through the use of environmental resources. The personality also interprets social needs and guides a person's efforts to respond to them. Figure 2.1 demonstrates the interacting nature of the biological, psychological, sociostructural, and cultural dimensions of the personality system. It acknowledges the importance of hereditary factors as well as events in the social and physical world as significant behavioral determinants. In Figure 2.1, Kimmel (1980) conceptualizes the dynamic interaction between the individual and society on a private-public continuum. The "private" (darkly shaded) area represents those aspects of personality that are internal and inaccessible to others. Included in his discussion of "public" sources of behavior are cultural ideologies, the economic

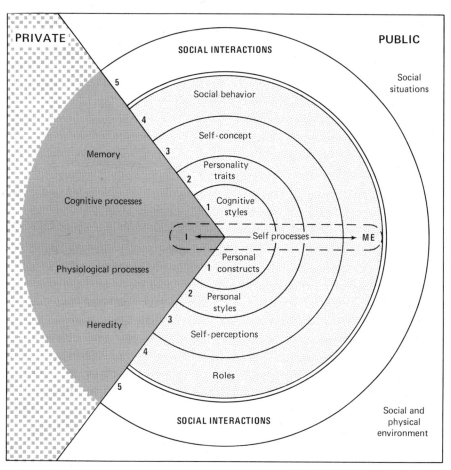

PRIVATE

PUBLIC

SOCIAL INTERACTIONS

Social situations

5

Social behavior

4

Self-concept

Memory

3

Personality traits

2

Cognitive processes

Cognitive styles

1

(I ← ——— Self processes ——— → M E)

Physiological processes

Personal constructs 1

Personal styles 2

Heredity

Self-perceptions 3

4

Roles

5

SOCIAL INTERACTIONS

Social and physical environment

FIGURE 2.1—The Holistic Quality of Human Behavior

system, and social norms. Change introduced in any of these external influences brings about the corresponding change in one's physiological state. Fricke's (1981) account of growing up as a homosexual provides an excellent example of how biological and psychological development are strongly influenced by external forces that may disadvantage and hurt members of minority groups. As a system of interacting biological, psychological, social-structural, and cultural components, the human being is very complex. The larger systems created by the interaction of great numbers of people become even more complex. Before turning to the concepts that focus on these larger systems,

TABLE 2.2—A SUMMARY OF BASIC PSYCHOLOGICAL CONCEPTS	
Cognition	Perception
Conditioning	Personality
Emotion (affect)	Psychological defenses
Motivation	Socialization

Table 2.2 summarizes basic psychological concepts, each of which you should be able to define briefly but accurately.

Basic Social-structural Concepts

Social-structure, or **social organization,** refers to the ways in which social behavior becomes patterned and predictable. Underlying the concept of social structure is the belief that social behavior is, for the most part, organized and non-random. Several kinds of patterning occur. **Social institutions** are especially important parts of the social structure, organizing activities around particular social purposes or functions. For example, as a social institution the family organizes categories of people— fathers, husbands, wives, sons, daughters, cousins, mothers-in-law, and so forth—around the performance of functions essential to the survival of society. Reproduction, socialization and care of the young, education, primary group relationships, and decision making about economic resources are examples of these important functions. Other social institutions include education, religion, politics, economics, and social welfare. Each of these organizes the behavior of large numbers of people around social functions. These institutions are closely related to each other, and introducing change in one institutional structure usually necessitates a corresponding change in the other structures. The changing role of women, for instance, directly affects not only the family institution, but the religious, political, and economic institutions as well.

Role refers to the expected behavior of categories of people within social institutions: the role of mothers, the role of sons, and so on. Most people participate in many social institutions and occupy many roles at the same time. Sometimes the demands of these multiple roles conflict and cause difficulty for people who are attempting to perform them. Again, using the example of the changing roles of women, societal expectations have changed dramatically in the past few decades. With these changes have come corresponding changes in the behavior of individual women and men. While the concept of role explains the predictability of much social behavior, occupying multiple roles simultaneously (mother, executive, wife) often produces **role conflict,** wherein the effective performance of one role may be in direct conflict with the effective performance of others. Another problem occurs when the behavioral expectations within a specific role are inconsistent. This is referred to as **role strain** as, for example, when parents are expected to provide nurturance and discipline, yet experience these activities as somewhat incompatible.

The functions, or purposes, of social institutions are often partly **manifest** (publicly stated and assumed to be for the good of society as a whole) and partly **latent** (less public and more beneficial for some groups in society than for others). For example, the manifest function of social welfare as a social institution is to provide basic resources for those who lack them. However, the point is often made that the latent function is to control people (especially minority groups and the poor) by manipulating the resources they receive and the ways they are made available. In part this relates to the nature of interaction among people and groups in a social structure. **Cooperative** interaction maximizes the focus on the good of society as a whole, whereas **competitive** interaction encourages people to focus on their own good. **Conflict** can carry competition into the realm of actively destructive behavior by one group in relation to others.

Social structures rarely treat everyone equally. Usually there is some type of **social differentiation** in which criteria are used to distinguish between groups of people. Commonly used criteria are age, sex, race, ethnicity, and physical characteristics such as size, looks, and the presence of physical handicaps. While such differentiation can be used simply to relate ability to activity— children are not allowed to drive because they lack the ability to do so, for example—it may also be used to stratify people. **Social stratification** refers to the process of ranking people in terms of socially defined criteria. A stratification process is a type of hierarchy, a vertical arrangement of people on the basis of access to resources. In a stratification system, some people are considered more important than others. This lays the foundation for discrimination and prejudice. **Discrimination** involves acts that disadvantage people who are considered less worthy. They are based on **prejudice,** beliefs that attribute negative characteristics to people without any concrete evidence to support these beliefs. An example of discrimination would be sending minority group children to low-quality segregated schools because of prejudice about the intelligence of members of minority groups.

Those with access to resources usually have power. **Power** is the ability of a person or group to enforce its will on others and it may be based on **authority** (legitimate power) or illegitimate **coercion,** or force. The importance of power is the control it confers over resources that are socially defined as valuable. There is, then, a reciprocal relationship between power and access to resources. Resources can include practically anything—money, diamonds, gold, food, reputation, goat skins, old furniture, physical size or appearance, land, weapons, and on and on. Those in power control the decision making that establishes the policies determining the production and distribution of many socially desirable resources.

Access to basic life-sustaining resources is essential for survival. Such resources are made available through the economic institution, which has as its major social function extracting natural resources from the environment, producing goods from them, distributing those goods, and providing needed services. These functions are performed through the use of land, labor, capital, entrepreneurship, and technology. Those with power have more control over and access to economic processes. Therefore, these have more goods and services, as well as decision-making power to protect their privileged position. In our own society, access to money is the single most important factor in ensuring access to basic life-sustaining resources. The poor have little money and thus limited ability to get the resources they need. Limited life-sustaining resources may threaten life itself, or reduce the quality of life. That is why poor people experience higher rates of disease, death, crime, social isolation, unemployment, and low levels of schooling. **Poverty,** then, is the chronic lack of life-sustaining and life-enriching resources. **Social class** is the category in which the stratification process places people according to their access to such life-sustaining and life-enriching resources.

To understand poverty and social class, two factors are especially important. One is the very nature of economic processes. When problems occur in the relationships between the use of land, labor, capital, entrepreneurship, and technology, large-scale economic problems are likely to result. This is what happens during recessions and depressions, affecting people at all social class levels (although the poor are generally affected first and most severely). The second factor is social differentiation. When social differentiation is tied to social stratification, a situation is created in which power is used by some groups (the dominant or majority groups) to maintain their own privilege (access to resources) at the expense of other groups (minority groups). Dominant in our own society are men, those of Western European backgrounds, Caucasians, the rich, and heterosexuals, while women, other racial and ethnic groups,[3] the poor, the elderly, those with physical deficits, and homosexuals are minorities. Membership in a minority group increases the likelihood that one's resources will be limited. For example, women and blacks are discriminated against when seeking high-paying and prestigious jobs (or, for that matter, graduate education to prepare for such jobs). We can see, then, that there is a clear relationship among social differentiation, social stratification, power, and access to socially desirable resources. Concepts and principles learned in the disciplines of sociology, economics, and political science have direct utility for the human service professional. Working effectively with people requires the ability to comprehend how these forces operate together to shape the context of human behavior.

One last correlate of power and social differentiation is important for human service professionals to understand—**social control.** This refers to the procedures used by a social structure to

---

[3]A race is a large population group that shares hereditary characteristics passed down from generation to generation. An ethnic group is a population group which shares a culture, although it may also have some common hereditary characteristics.

maintain order, because disorder threatens the structure itself. Naturally, those persons who occupy positions of power are concerned with preserving the existing social structure because they benefit most from it. Those who have limited access to social resources and who feel they cannot increase their access may believe they have little to lose by challenging the existing social structure. Hence, social control mechanisms are often seen as repressive by minority group members. Social control mechanisms include socialization (teaching people only socially acceptable ways to behave), **social sanctions** (socially defined positive or negative responses to behavior), and physical force such as is vested in the criminal justice system.

As is probably obvious, social structures organize individual behavior through groups. A **group** is two or more people who have a sense of common purpose and interact on a regular basis. There are many kinds of groups and many specific aspects of group structure that affect the behavior of group members (decision making, leadership, group purpose, and so forth). Of particular significance is whether a group is primary or secondary. A **primary group** is generally small and is characterized by intensive, face-to-face interaction. Primary groups may be goal-directed at times, but they are also structures for meeting the basic needs of their members for acceptance and care. **Secondary groups** are larger and generally more impersonal, and focused more on goal attainment than on meeting members' basic needs. Especially important secondary groups are **formal organizations** or **bureaucracies.** These group structures have goals that are clearly identified, as well as specified means for attaining these goals. They also have a hierarchical structure of relationships, an emphasis on jobs or positions rather than the specific people who perform the jobs at any particular time, and the expectation that interaction between members will be around performing the job rather than personal wishes or needs.

Formal organizations dominate a society like our own. Indeed, most social welfare services are provided through such structures. Therefore, it is important for service providers and anyone seeking help to learn how to function effectively in formal organizations. The demands can be severe, because the emphasis is on job perfomance rather than meeting personal needs for acceptance, creative outlets, freedom of choice, and so on.

Primary groups, therefore, are important antidotes to the strains of large-scale secondary groups like formal organizations, because primary groups do allow the expression of personal needs. One frequent source of tension for the professional employed in large formal organizations is the apparent inconsistency between the goals of the organization (efficiency, for instance) and the belief in service to people. The inability to deal effectively with these incompatible goals is a common source of professional burn-out.

Social structure, then, determines how resources will be made available, and to whom. Groups mediate between the individual and the social structure as a whole. Linking back to earlier sections, we can see how biology generates potential that is developed through psychological means and enriched or restricted in the environment managed by the social structure. Nurturing environments encourage psychological growth and development consistent with biological potentials. Political climates support or inhibit the development of social structures that form the context for human behavior. By way of example, we will now look at hunger in America to see how political decisions affect biological and psychological well-being.

Hunger in America. Political and economic realities serve as important influences on behavior, but as with other social-structural variables, their impact is often not directly observed by practitioners. The political issue of hunger in America is a case in point. The Citizen's Commission on Hunger in New England (1984) contends that hunger is the result of conscious government policies. A similar conclusion is reported by Senator Edward Kennedy (1983) in his report to the Committee on Labor and Human Resources of the United States Senate entitled *Going Hungry in America*. The report states that at a time when record numbers of Americans were enduring severe economic deprivation due to the recession of 1981-1982, simultaneous cut-backs in federal nutrition and other food assistance programs were occurring.

Reductions in the Food Stamp program, in child nutrition programs, and in Aid to Families with Dependent Children (AFDC) payment levels are all examples of social policy decisions that directly affect the quality of life of an increasingly large population of Americans. Both the New England and the Kennedy reports further conclude that hunger in America is a problem that can be solved, given a realignment of national priorities. Our hunger is not because of lack of food—government policies actually provide incentives for farmers to limit food production, thereby creating an obstacle from a natural resource.

Dietary deficiency diseases, neonatal and infant mortality rates, low birth weights, failure-to-thrive syndrome are all health-related (biological) phenomena, significantly connected with social-structural and cultural variables. Not only does the social-structural condition of prolonged deprivation negatively affect one's biological growth and development, it also adversely affects one's emotional life and sense of hope. The New England report found that formerly stable families were destroyed by economic hardship and concluded that "hunger and poverty . . . set in motion a deterioration and destabilization of once strong individuals, families, and neighborhoods" (Citizen's Commission on Hunger in New England, 1984, p. 16).

The example of hunger in America serves to illustrate the interrelatedness of biological, psychological, social-structural, and cultural phenomena in explaining the complex nature of human behavior in the social environment. Exhibit 5.2 at the end of Chapter 5 presents a portrait of one family as it struggles to

---

TABLE 2.3—A SUMMARY OF
BASIC SOCIAL-STRUCTURAL CONCEPTS

Authority	Power
Bureaucracy (formal organization)	Prejudice
Coercion	Primary group
Competition	Role
Conflict	Role strain
Cooperation	Secondary group
Discrimination	Social class
Dominant (majority) group	Social control
Group	Social differentiation
Latent functions	Social institutions
Manifest functions	Social sanction
Minority group	Social stratification
Poverty	Social structure (social organization)

survive amidst economic hardship and hunger. It painfully illustrates the psychological effects of deprivation. Table 2.3 summarizes the basic social-structural concepts discussed in this section to help you review your command of each.

Basic Cultural Concepts

When we think most broadly about our environment, we usually think of society. However, culture is even broader than society. **Culture** is the storehouse of values, knowledge, and material objects that a group has accumulated and preserved over generations. **Society** is a group of people who share a geographical area in which a particular culture is used and made operational through a social structure. Using our own society as an example, we can clearly identify the geographical boundaries of the United States. We can also describe the values, ways of doing things, and technology characteristic of our society as a whole. For example, we do not sacrifice virgins to deities, we speak our own version of English—somewhat different from the English spoken in Great Britain—we drive on the right side of the road, we generally find nuclear energy acceptable, and most of us like air conditioning when it is hot. Aspects of our culture are translated into specific behaviors, rules for behavior, and organizational procedures that characterize our day-to-day behavior in this society.

It is clear that there are variations within a culture in the way people think and act. This is due to **subcultures,** smaller groups existing within the large group that have some unique cultural characteristics. Italian Americans, for example, have different values and behaviors with respect to the family than do Native Americans. It is important for the social welfare professional to keep in mind, however, that even within subcultures there is a great deal of intragroup variation. It is unsafe to assume that any individual member of a group will behave in ways consistent with the predominant patterns attributed to the subculture with which he/she identifies. One common error of beginning practitioners is to apply generalizations that are shared by most members of a cultural group to an individual within that group. To assume, therefore, that because someone is a first-generation migrant from Appalachia, s/he will behave in a set, predictable fashion will often be incorrect because the assumption is based on a stereotype. Members of cultural groups generally share certain beliefs, values, and behaviors, but each individual combines these in unique ways that reflect his/her particular situation.

Subcultures usually coexist in such a way as to preserve the structure of the larger culture of which they are a part. This harmonious coexistence of different subcultural groups is called **cultural pluralism.** Cultural pluralism recognizes the legitimacy of the traditions of diverse subcultures. Cultural diversity, viewed with a pluralist lens, is seen as a resource to be encouraged. As a pattern of racial and ethnic relations, cultural pluralism is in contrast to the **melting pot** philosophy, which traditionally characterized American society. Fusion of all diverse racial and ethnic subcultures into one "American blend" is the goal of the melting pot theory of race and ethnic relations. When one subcultural (or cultural) group questions the appropriateness of the way another culture is structured, or evaluates another group on the basis of its own cultural elements, then **ethnocentrism** is occurring. Social workers and others working with people have to remember that the cultural integrity of each subcultural group is the only appropriate context for understanding that group's behavior. That some elements of a subculture may create difficulties for its members in the larger culture does not mean either group is right or wrong. Careful negotiation is required to see that the needs of both groups are met in ways appropriate for each.

Ethnocentrism is sometimes the cause of definitions of deviance. A culture's, or subculture's, values generate **norms,** or rules of behavior. Behavior that violates these norms is considered unacceptable or **deviant.** Once again, it is important to note that behavior can only be judged acceptable or unacceptable when it is evaluated according to some standard. When groups have different standards, created by differences in their cultures, they may have difficulty accepting each other's behavior. For example, management of time in many Hispanic and black subcultures may be different from that in the dominant culture. This sometimes leads members of the dominant group to accuse Hispanics and blacks of being deviant by being late for appointments or unconcerned about "efficiency." Obviously, there is nothing inherently right or wrong about any group's management of time. It is only right or wrong with respect to some standard, and different cultural/subcultural groups often have different standards, or norms. The concept of **cultural relativity** means that any given aspect of culture must be evaluated within the context of the culture (and the historical period) in which it occurs. Attempts to apply universal standards of behavior to all situations are the result of ethnocentric thinking patterns. Clearly, power becomes a relevant factor in these situations, because the dominant group may attempt to impose its standards on others. Social welfare professionals need to be constantly vigilant so as to avoid this tendency.

Power conflicts are often couched in terms of right and wrong, which is simply another way of saying normative and deviant. Although a group with power may be able to label another group deviant, and persecute or otherwise control it as a result, the practitioner must be able to separate ethnocentrism from cultural pluralism. Whether or not one is successful in helping a minority group avoid being labeled and treated as deviant, s/he should at least be clear that there is nothing inherently wrong with a particular group's behavior. When discussing biological concepts, it was noted that difference is built into humans through the genetic process. Culture also builds in difference through the creation of alternatives in social behavior. However, a dominant group's definitions of normal and deviant may ignore these quite natural sources of difference. Short men may be devalued even though size is a natural biological variation. Similarly, sexually active women in one subculture may be stigmatized, whereas in other cultures and subcultures they may be accepted (Schur, 1984). The effect of culture on biological, psychological, and social-structural functioning is illustrated in Exhibit 2.1 at the end of the chapter, while Table 2.4 summarizes basic cultural concepts for you.

TABLE 2.4—A SUMMARY OF BASIC CULTURAL CONCEPTS

Culture	Melting pot theory
Cultural pluralism	Norms
Deviance	Society
Ethnocentrism	Subculture

Culture is a powerful influence on behavior because it serves to organize a society's social structure, which in turn governs people's actions. Once again we come back to the continuum from biological through cultural behavior. Human behavior is an interlocking whole in which each source influences the others. Although we begin our analysis of behavior in any of the four sources, sooner or later we must place it in its larger context. If we fail to do so, we have not looked at the question holistically and will therefore have difficulty focusing on the purpose of interventions to help people function more effectively in their environment. Each concept discussed in this section helps us understand some particular part of human behavior. Each deserves careful study, here and in the context of its respective discipline. But how are they all to be interrelated to become useful, practical tools for attaining the purposes of the helping professions? The next section will address the need to relate all of these concepts to each other so that practice is supported by a holistic view of human behavior.

As we stated in the beginning of this chapter, no attempt was made to exhaust all of the concepts the professional needs to understand in order to work effectively with people. What we have presented, however, are selected concepts that, when viewed in context, are helpful to the generalist practitioner in a variety of social welfare settings. The chapter will conclude with a framework that will help the professional pull together selected concepts in a way that is useful in developing a holistic viewpoint.

THE INTEGRATING FRAMEWORK

Human behavior is a whole in which some parts are initiated and maintained biologically, others psychologically, and still others socially and culturally. Professionals need to view the practice situations they encounter in a way that incorporates these four sources of behavior. Such a view must focus on the holistic quality of human behavior at the same time that it recognizes the many different ways that the biological, psychological, social, and cultural components of that behavior can be put together by people to identify and strive toward life goals. Figure 2.2 presents a diagram of how this practice might look.

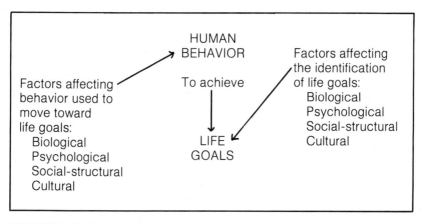

FIGURE 2.2—Human Behavior and Professional Practice

In order to make informed decisions about how to intervene in a practice situation, the practitioner must understand the relationship between all the parts of the situation shown in Figure 2.2.

When we talk about biological, psychological, social-structural, and cultural factors affecting human behavior and efforts to identify and achieve life goals, we must recognize that these factors can either serve as resources or as obstacles. For example, biological factors influencing behavior serve as *resources* when they facilitate poeple's ability to achieve life goals. When they inhibit the realization of life goals (as in certain illnesses and other pathological states) they become *obstacles.* At the species level, humans utilize a wide variety of adaptive behaviors when attempting to satisfy a need. At the individual level, high intelligence enables a person to learn quickly how to analyze and understand complex situations. On the other hand, these same factors can be obstacles when they make it more difficult for people to achieve life goals. Because humans have few genetically programmed reflexes, they are heavily dependent on each other for physical care and social learning. Those people who are isolated from others for social or biological reasons, or who have few opportunities to learn from others are severely restricted in their efforts to identify and move toward life goals. Similarly, people of high intelligence may actually be at a disadvantage in situations requiring the strict observance of rules and the performance of highly routinized activities.

How can a social welfare professional best analyze the biological, psychological, social-structural, and cultural sources of
behavior to understand when and how they function as resources
and obstacles? A three-part framework is an aid to accomplishing
this task. Looking at a situation holistically enables us to examine
how its various components interact in ways that create resources, obstacles, or both. We will use a *systems* perspective[4] to
provide us with such a holistic view. Secondly, we can focus on
ways that biologically and socially created differences affect the
manner in which situations are perceived and experienced by
different people. This helps us to understand how similar
biological, psychological, social-structural, and cultural factors
become resources for some and obstacles for others. We will use a
human diversity perspective to make us alert to the sources and
effects of such differences. Third, seeing human behavior as
goal-directed aids us in our search for order and patterns in
human behavior that sometimes seems highly idiosyncratic and
even illogical. Resources and obstacles can then be analyzed in
terms of human purpose as defined by the actors in social
situations themselves. We will use *goal-directed behavior* as a
perspective that maintains our focus on purpose. These relationships can be diagrammed as shown in Figure 2.3.

The framework that helps pull together the various dimensions
of behavior is built upon systems, human diversity, and goal-
directed behavior. When analyzing a practice situation, this
framework directs the practitioner to examine the systems
involved, the elements of diversity involved, and the goal being
sought. In order to apply these three perspectives to a practice
situation, a worker, for instance, needs to be aware of the
biological, psychological, social-structural, and cultural components of each. By using the three perspectives and the sources of
behavior together, the resources and obstacles existing or poten-

[4]*Perspective* is being used in this book according to Anne Minahan's definition:
"Perspectives are ways to think about and visualize situations." Her analysis of
the difference between theories, perspectives, and concepts is very helpful, and
is recommended to the reader. See Anne Minahan, "Theories and perspectives
for social work," *Social Work,* 25 (6), November 1980, p. 435.

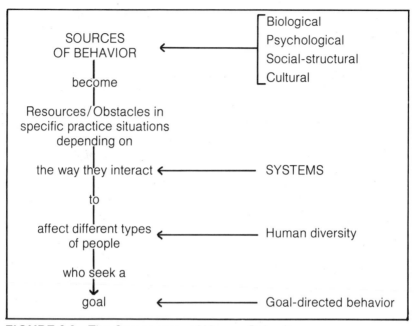

FIGURE 2.3—The Components of Human Behavior

tially available in a practice situation can be identified. For example, let us consider helping parents who have abused their children. We will use the systems perspective to see why helping them develop more effective parenting skills is one possible interventive strategy. Biological characteristics of the parent or children could be a significant source of stress which might lead to abusive behavior. A hyperactive child may make demands on parents which they feel unable to meet. A parent suffering from malnutrition may lack the energy necessary to perform even minimal parenting tasks. In both cases, child abuse may be used to control the child's behavior so that it is seen as manageable by the struggling parent. In this example, biological characteristics are tied to their causes (such as inadequate nutrition) as well as their social behavior (child abuse). The holistic perspective, therefore, has helped to identify significant biological characteristics of a situation in order to better understand how they interact with other aspects of that situation. A more holistic view results. Existing or potential resources and obstacles are also easier to identify. If inadequate nutrition is an obstacle to effective parenting, financial, medical, and educational services are some of the resources needed to help solve the problem. To understand such a practice situation in its totality, the human diversity and goal-directed behavior perspectives would also have to be applied. These will be developed in the following chapters.

The framework being proposed uses knowledge in an integrated manner to understand practice situations holistically, and it is diagrammed in Table 2.5. It is important to remember that all three perspectives are critical to a holistic view of any practice situation.

SUMMARY

This chapter has presented an overview of the biological, psychological, social-structural, and cultural dimensions of human behavior. Selected concepts from the biological, social, and behavioral sciences that are useful to the social welfare professional have been reviewed. The chapter concluded with a framework that will help the beginning practitioner pull together these multiple sources of behavior into a holistic view of professional practice. The goal of professional practice is improving the transactions between people and environments. Knowledge geared toward understanding the factors influencing these transactions comes from several disciplines and demands of the practitioner the ability to select, integrate, and apply information from diverse sources. The next two chapters will focus on how the components in Table 2.5 (systems, human diversity, and goal-directed behavior) aid our understanding of human behavior. In later chapters, the framework for applying knowledge in a holistic way will be used within the context of the life cycle.

STUDY QUESTIONS

1. About which of the four sources of behavior (biological, psychological, social-structural, and cultural) do you feel most knowledgeable? Why do you know more about some than about the others? Does this tell you something about cultural values, education as a social institution, and your own interests and

TABLE 2.5—FRAMEWORK FOR USING KNOWLEDGE TO UNDERSTAND PRACTICE SITUATIONS HOLISTICALLY

Sources of behavior and their situational effects

Perspectives for a holistic view	*Biological*		*Psychological*		*Social-structural*		*Cultural*	
	RESOURCE	OBSTACLE	RESOURCE	OBSTACLE	RESOURCE	OBSTACLE	RESOURCE	OBSTACLE
SYSTEMS								
HUMAN DIVERSITY								
GOAL-DIRECTED BEHAVIOR								

experiences? How committed are you to expanding your knowledge in those areas in which you are presently less knowledgeable? How might you do so?

2. When are you most likely to consciously assess your
resources? Have you ever thought of them as including biological,
psychological, social-structural, and cultural components? Thinking of them in this way, do you consider that you have more or
fewer resources than you had previously thought? How about
obstacles—do you see more or less of these in your life using the
framework presented in this chapter?

3. Thinking about obstacles again, identify one group of people
for each type of obstacle (that is, biological, psychological, social-
structural, and cultural) whom you feel have the most serious of
that type of obstacle to overcome. Explain what these obstacles
are and why you consider them especially important in terms of
their effects on the lives of the people involved. Do you think
others would agree with your selection of the groups with the
most severe obstacles? Why or why not? Finally, can you also
identify resources each group might use in coping with the
obstacles you have identified?

4. Carel Germain (1979) states that the professional purpose
of social work "arises from a dual, simultaneous concern for the
adaptive potential of people and the nutritive qualities of their
environment." Calling this an "ecological approach," she elabor-
ates by pointing out that it is "concerned with the growth,
development, and potentialities of human beings and with the
properties of their environment that support or fail to support the
expression of human potential." Why do you think Germain
would have chosen the concept of ecology as the best one to use
when examining transactions between people and the environment? What other concepts could she have used? Having
analyzed the alternatives, do you think she made a wise choice?

5. Thinking in terms of transaction suggests an exchange
between the parties involved. Why is this an important part of our
thinking as professionals about the relationships people have
with their environment? Use examples of real-life situations to
support your answer. What are the different implications for
helping if people do or do not engage in transactions/exchanges
with their environment?

6. Read Exhibit 2.1 at the end of the chapter. How do you react to this article? Is it consistent with your observations? Do you see any change in the behavioral patterns of men and women in terms of aggression? What are the relative influences of biology, culture, and social-structure on male/female aggression?

KEY TERMS

Affect   The feelings that become attached to information derived from perceptions and cognitive functioning.

Authority   Power recognized as legitimate by those it affects.

Bureaucracy   A specific type of formal organization. It is characterized by fixed rules, hierarchial authority structures, and specialized functions.

Chromosome   A body within the nucleus of a cell that carries the genes that determine a structure or characteristic.

Coercion   Illegitimate power based in force.

Cognition   The ability to process and organize sensory information in order to manipulate the environment to achieve one's goals.

Cultural pluralism   A form of minority-majority relation in which diversity is applauded.

Cultural relativity   Evaluating elements of a culture within the context of the culture in which they occur.

Culture   The entire way of life of a people, including values, beliefs, behaviors, and artifacts that are transmitted from generation to generation.

Defenses   Psychological mechanisms such as projection, denial, and rationalization that help the personality keep a balance between the desires of the individual and the demands of the society.

Deviance   Any behavior that violates societal expectations.

Discrimination   Acts that disadvantage people considered less worthy, and which result from prejudice.

Explanatory knowledge   Knowledge that seeks to explain behavior, but not necessarily alter it.

Ethnocentrism   The tendency to consider the norms and values of one's group as being superior to those of other groups.

Formal organization   A complex social structure that is deliberately organized to achieve specific goals.

Group   Two or more people who have a sense of common purpose and interact on a regular basis.

Intervention knowledge   Knowledge that seeks to predict, control, or change behavior.

Labeling theory   A theory of deviant behavior that asserts deviance is the result of one group successfully applying the label of deviant to another group.

Latent functions   Functions of a social institution that are often unintended, but nonetheless powerful.

Life chances   Access to material resources that affects one's life experiences.

Manifest functions   Those functions of social institutions that are commonly accepted by most members of the society.

Melting pot   Fusing diverse racial and ethnic subcultures into one culture.

Minority group   Any group with limited access to social power.

Norms   Cultural standards that define appropriate and inappropriate behavior.

Perception   The ability to see, hear, smell, feel, and touch, and to develop organized responses to selected sensory characteristics of the environment.

Personality   The integrating psychological structure that develops to help the individual function in society. Consistent patterns of behavior that differentiate people from each other.

Poverty   The chronic lack of life-sustaining and life-enriching resources.

Power   The ability to control resources and policy making, thereby leading to the ability to control the behavior of others.

Prejudice   Beliefs that attribute negative characteristics to people without any concrete evidence to support these beliefs.

Primary group   A small group characterized by extensive, face-to-face interaction.

Role   Expected attitudes and behaviors accompanying a given social position.

Role conflict   A problem encountered when an individual attempts to perform two or more incompatible roles.

Role strain A problem encountered when there are inconsistencies within a given role.

Secondary group A large group characterized by impersonal interaction and a focus on goal attainment.

Social class The category in which people are placed through the stratification process based on similarity of access to life-sustaining and life-enriching resources.

Social control The procedures used by a social structure to maintain order.

Social differentiation Distinguishing among groups of people according to socially-determined criteria.

Social sanctions Socially defined responses to behavior; they may be positive (approval) or negative (disapproval).

Socialization The process by which one internalizes the norms and values of a society.

Society A geographical area in which a particular culture is used and made operational through a social structure.

Social structure The institutions, roles, and categories of status that serve to organize social behavior.

Sociobiology The study of the biological base of social behavior.

Subculture A subgroup of the dominant culture that establishes its own values and norms that distinguish it from the dominant culture.

This chapter has explored the biological, psychological, social-structural, and cultural sources of behavior. The fact that these four behavioral dimensions interact is a significant part of the chapter's message. The two exhibits that follow illustrate this fact. The first looks at the biological and psychological phenomenon of aggression. Aggression is shown to be related to physical size and strength (biological), but also to the way men and women are taught to perceive their place in the world around them. Most men are taught, through social-structural arrangements, to incorporate aggression into their personalities (psychological). Women are less frequently taught to behave in this way.

The second exhibit looks at cultural definitions of the elderly and of aging. It shows how cultural beliefs get translated into social-structural arrangements that serve to make the beliefs come true. This occurs even though studies have shown that there are few biological reasons why most elderly people have to severly limit their participation in societal affairs. Both exhibits, then, make the point that social definitions of appropriate behavior become important influences on how people develop biologically and psychologically.

2.1: GENDER AND AGGRESSION

While psychologists and psychiatrists often disagree sharply when they discuss whether behavioral differences between the sexes exist, many agree on one difference—that boys and men are still the more aggressive and violent. Nevertheless, the subject of aggression continues to produce heated conversation.

Part of the reason for the battle over whether or not males are more aggressive is semantic. Many social scientists use a specific definition of aggression—physical or verbal behavior that hurts or seems intended to hurt other people. In popular usage, however, "aggressive" is often used to describe qualities such as assertiveness, competitiveness and ambition. These quality do not necessarily involve harm to others and may have no automatic connection with aggression. In their recent research into sexual differences, social scientists have focused on aggression as harmful behavior. What follows are some of their findings.

The difference between aggressive behavior in the sexes is significant. "The greater aggressiveness of the male is one of the best established and

continued

most pervasive, of all psychological sex differences," wrote Dr. Eleanore E. Maccoby and Dr. Carol Nagy Jacklin, Stanford University psychologists who are among the leading experts on sex differences. They cited psychological experiments that have shown men are consistently more likely to administer what they think to be high levels of electric shock to other research subjects.

Differences Found Worldwide

Sharply varying rates of aggression between the sexes can be seen in societies all over the world. "I don't know of any society where females do more aggressive acts than males or any society where females commit as much aggression," said Dr. Napoleon Chagnon, a professor of anthropology at Northwestern University and a well-known researcher in the field.

The differences in male and female aggression can be seen early in life. Dr. Maccoby and Dr. Jacklin say that greater male aggression begins to be evident by the time children begin social play at 2 or 2½ years old.

Although a greater proportion of aggressive behavior by females is verbal, males are characterized by more spoken as well as physical aggression. While some males do attack females, most male aggression is directed against other males.

Female physical aggression, whether directed against spouses, children or siblings, is more likely to take place in the home. Social scientists say that women kill their husbands at about the same rate as men kill their wives, although many of these women kill in self-defense.

As women move into a more equal status in the United States, according to Dr. Freda Adler, a Rutgers University professor of criminal justice, aggressive crime by women is increasing, but men are still arrested for violent crimes about nine times more often than women.

Most People Control Aggression

Most members of both sexes effectively control their aggression. While there are more highly aggressive men, the difference in aggression between the average man and the average women is not great.

Aggressive people are often not effective in protecting their own interests. Dr. Gerald R. Patterson, a psychologist at the Oregon Social Learning Center in Portland, said that the aggressive, antisocial boys he treats are usually beaten when they provoke other boys. "They are not very good fighters," he said.

Many behavioral scientists say that aggression is usually personally and socially destructive. Others argue that it can be useful, is occasionally mobilized

continued

for self-defense and, in any case, is inescapable.

"Aggression is and always will be here," said Dr. Eleanor Galenson, a clinical professor of psychiatry at the Mount Sinai School of Medicine in Manhattan.

While many behavioral scientists find that males are more aggressive, they say the evidence is much less clear about whether males as a group are more competitive or assertive. "You have to distinguish between assertiveness and aggression; there is a low correlation between them," said Arnold H. Buss, a psychology professor at the University of Texas at Austin. Dr. Buss pointed out that assertive people are not necessarily aggressive.

Dr. Maccoby and Dr. Jacklin have written that their examination of the scientific literature on competitiveness indicates that many studies "usually show boys to be more competitive, but there are many studies finding sex similarity."

Women as Achievers

Dr. Maccoby said in an interview that she found no reason to believe that women had less desire to achieve important positions but because they had been taught to be more sensitive to the feelings of others, women often had less interest in competition that involved trying to best someone else.

While the difference in aggressiveness or hurtful behavior seems to have a biological basis, which many scientists relate to the presence of the male hormone testosterone, there is no evident biological component in such personality traits as assertiveness and competitiveness, Dr. Maccoby and other behavioral scientists say. Furthermore, they contend that such traits are heavily influenced by the child's social learning. If women are less competitive or less aggressive, what they have learned is acceptable behavior from family, other adults and peers is of great importance.

There are indications that differing parental conceptions and socialization in relation to physical activity and aggression may start very early. Dr. Paula J. Caplan, an assistant professor of psychiatry at the University of Toronto, cites studies indicating that adults identify newborn babies as heavier and more active when they are told they are boys than when the same babies are described as girls.

Adults Often Rough With Boys

Behavioral scientists also point to the greater willingness of adults to engage in rough-and-tumble play with boys, to tolerate their rough behavior and to use physical discipline on them. They also note that parents and other adults are much more likely to tell a boy to fight back when he is picked on; a girl may be told to walk away from the

continued

situation or report it to a teacher or other adult.

While boys can be taught that aggression is not always a bad thing, Dr. Caplan says that girls are taught to suppress aggression because of their role in child-rearing and the undesirability of expressing aggression toward children. Dr. Maccoby and Dr. Jacklin suggest that the female's child-bearing and child-rearing role may also cause adults to watch girls more closely and to train them more in nurturing behavior.

Some Families Try to Change

With the rise in expectations for equality of opportunity for women, some families have tried to change child-rearing practices to diminish sex differentiation. In addition, behavioral scientists have reconsidered their views.

"We have seen how our conception of gender differences has changed under the influence of the women's movement," said Dr. Anke A. Ehrhardt, professor of clinical psychology at Columbia University's College of Physicians and Surgeons. He noted that women in numbers have proved themselves able to fill the jobs once thought to be performable only by men.

Whether in aggression, violence or constructive forms of competition, scholars look for social conditions to narrow what have been perceived as disparities between the sexes. "The differences may not be as great as the figures indicate," said Dr. Richard F. Sparks, a Rutgers behavioral scientist. "And the females are slowly closing the gap."

—SOURCE: Bryce Nelson, "Aggression: Still a Stronger Trait for Males." The New York Times, June 20, 1983, p. B6.

2.2: PEOPLE OUT TO PASTURE

Age 65 is obsolete. It has become an anachronism as a basis of policy, as a result of improved health and startling increases in longevity for many Americans. And yet the prevailing belief is that age 65 has some special significance. In this view, people are just late middle-aged until they reach their 65th birthday, at which time they suddenly are considered elderly.

Age 65 is no longer a realistic dividing line between the middle-aged and elderly. The great majority of Americans don't age significantly until they are well into their 70's. On balance, they are still vigorous, sound of mind and body and tend to lead active, contributing lives. They are not at all like the elderly of earlier times, when nearly anyone who reached the age of 65 really was old.

But, someone will say, did we not raise the legal retirement age of 70? Yes, we did, but that act of political expediency had little significance for most Americans. The participation of older people in the labor force has continued to decline, partly as a result of personal choice but also because of the pervasive myths that encourage it.

The mystique of age 65 obscures a growing contradiction between the increased longevity and vigor of older Americans and attitudes and policies that encourage increasingly early retirement. We forbid discrimination in employment on account of age and say, at least publicly, that our aim is to keep people in the labor force as long as possible. And yet we allow Social Security benefits to be drawn at age 62 and impose a penalty on beneficiaries under the age of 72 who exceed the allowable earned income. Privately, many employers, through a subtle combination of pressure and financial inducement, are getting rid of older workers to make way for less senior, less costly and allegedly more adaptable younger workers.

We need to rethink our attitudes toward retirement age so that public and private-business policies for older Americans are better attuned to the realities of our time.

I propose a concept that might be called the "third quarter" of life, which embraces people from the ages of 50 to 75. While such a notion may be somewhat startling in its assumption that most of us are likely to live to be 100, it makes far more sense from a policy standpoint than the arbitrary classification of pre- and post-65-year-olds.

For most people, the early 50's are a major turning point. Their children have grown up

continued

and left home, they have reached their maximum real earning power, are unlikely to be promoted again and are restless and often bored with their jobs. They need a major change of career—a "repotting," so to speak—to stimulate new interests that they can pursue well into their 70's. During that span, the chances are high that they will remain vigorous, healthy and mentally alert, and, if given the chance, will continue to be productive.

Does this mean that they should continue in full-time, paid employment for the entire third quarter? Not at all. That concept of productivity is also obsolete. In the future, the notion of productivity must be broadened to include part-time as well as full-time paid work and full- and part-time volunteer jobs. Most important, there must be a social expectation that people will remain productive throughout the third quarter of their lives and will be accepted by younger people as contributing, fully involved members of the community.

What is needed to enable third-quarter Americans to be productive in the broad sense is clear enough. First, society needs to look upon them as an asset, rather than a burden. Then, government and business should help them by providing equal access to retraining, phased retirement, greater flexibility in the use of both public and private pension benefits, greatly expanded public service employment similar to that presently existing under the Federal Senior Community Service Employment Program, and better organized volunteer jobs.

Some of these changes would cost money, but they would also produce substantial savings by using older people's skills, experience and reliability and by cutting health costs. The more active and productive their lives, the healthier they will be. And as older workers, through the challenge provided by new careers, begin to reverse the trend toward early retirement, the growing burden on the Social Security system will be eased.

There are 50 million third-quarter Americans today—more than a fifth of the population. In another three decades, there will be 85 million—nearly a third of the expected population at that time. As a nation, we have no choice but to become concerned about the productivity of these citizens. Their capacity to contribute to the general welfare in the years ahead is enormous. It must not be ignored.

—SOURCE: Alan Pifer, "Put Out to Pasture: Our Idea of Age 65."
The New York Times,
February 7, 1984.

ADDITIONAL READINGS

Coser, L. (1964). *The functions of social conflict.* New York: Free Press.

Coser, L., & Rosenberg, B. (Eds.). (1976). *Sociological theory* (4th ed.). New York: Macmillan.

Federico, R., & Schwartz, J. (1983). *Sociology* (3rd Ed.). Reading, MA: Addison-Wesley.

Gelfand, D. (1982). *The aging network: Programs and services* (2nd ed.). New York: Springer Publications.

Gouldner, A. (1970). *The coming crisis in Western sociology.* New York: Basic Books.

Hall, E. (1977). *Beyond culture.* Garden City, NY: Anchor Press.

Hall, W., & Young, C. (Eds.). (1977). *Genetic disorders: Social service interventions.* Pittsburgh: University of Pittsburgh Graduate School of Public Health.

Harris, M. (1974). *Cows, pigs, wars and witches: The riddles of culture.* New York: Vintage Books.

Harris, M. (1977). *Cannibals and kings: The origins of cultures.* New York: Random House.

Herand, B. (1970). *Sociology and social work.* Oxford: Pergamon Press.

Hilgard, E., & Bower, G. (1975). *Theories of learning.* Englewood Cliffs, NJ: Prentice-Hall.

Johnson, H. (1980). *Behavior, psychopathology, and the brain.* New York: Curriculum Concepts.

Katz, D., & Kahu, R.L. (1978). *The social psychology of organizations* (2nd ed.). New York: Wiley.

Lenski, G. (1970). *Human societies.* New York: McGraw-Hill.

Lidz, T. (1976). *The person: His and her development throughout the life cycle* (rev. ed.). New York: Basic Books.

Merton, R. (1968). *Social theory and social structure* (rev. ed.). New York: Free Press.

Mills, C.W. (1959). *The sociological imagination.* London: Oxford University Press.

Palmore, E. (1984). Longevity in Abkhazia: A reevaluation. *The Gerontologist, 24* (1), February.

Pellitier, K. (1977). *Mind as healer, mind as slayer: A holistic approach to preventing stress disorders.* New York: Delta Books.

Rose, A. (1967). *The power structure.* New York: Oxford University Press.

Ryan, W. (1972). *Blaming the victim.* New York: Random House.

Schiller, B. (1976). *The economics of poverty and discrimination* (2nd ed.).

Englewood Cliffs, NJ: Prentice-Hall.

Scott, J.W. (1982). The mechanization of women's work. *Scientific American, 247* (September), 167-187.

Strelen, H. (1975). *Personality theory and social work practice.* Metuchen, NJ: Scarecrow Press.

Tussing, A.D. (1975). *Poverty in a dual economy.* New York: St. Martin's Press.

Underwood, J. (1979). *Human variation and human micro evolution.* Englewood Cliffs, NJ: Prentice-Hall.

Warren, R. (1978). *The community in America* (3rd ed.). Chicago: Rand-McNally.

REFERENCES

Barash, D.P. (1977). *Sociobiology and behavior.* New York: Elsevier.

Citizens Commission on Hunger in New England. (1984). *American hunger crisis: Poverty and health in New England.* Boston: Harvard University School of Public Health.

Fricke, A. (1981). *Reflections of a rock lobster.* Boston: Alyson Publishing Company.

Gans, H. (1971). The uses of poverty: the poor pay all. *Social Policy* (July-August), 20-24.

Germain, C. (Ed.). (1979). *Social work practice: People and environments—an ecological approach* (p. 8). New York: Columbia University Press.

Kennedy, E.M. (1983). *Going hungry in America.* Report to the Committee on Labor and Human Resources, United States Senate, December 22.

Kimmel, D.C. (1980). *Adulthood and aging: An interdisciplinary, developmental view* (pp. 398-401). New York: Wiley.

Mendelsohn, A. (1980). *The work of social work* (p. 80). New York: New Viewpoints.

Schur, E.M. (1984). *Labeling women deviant: Gender, stigma, and social control.* New York: Random House.

3

INTEGRATING IDEAS: SYSTEMS, HUMAN DIVERSITY, AND GOAL-DIRECTED BEHAVIOR

- CHAPTER OVERVIEW
- SYSTEMS
  Definitions and Perspective
  The Human Body
  The Family
- CHARACTERISTICS OF SYSTEMS
  Boundaries
  Purpose
  Exchange
  Network

CHAPTER OVERVIEW

Chapter 2 presented the multifaceted dimensions of human behavior; reviewed specific concepts from the biological, social, and behavioral sciences; and ended by presenting a framework designed to help the generalist practitioner in using knowledge to understand practice situations holistically. This chapter will demonstrate how three components of that framework—systems, human diversity, and goal-directed behavior—can be used to accelerate the achievement of practice goals. Keep in mind that the overall objective of this text is to help you, as a generalist practitioner, to use knowledge about human behavior in the social environment. This chapter, then, builds on information presented in previous chapters and also serves as a base for material to be presented in subsequent chapters.

Definitions of systems will be presented, followed by a discussion of the characteristics of systems. A diagram will also be offered to illustrate how the various characteristics of systems are related. The chapter then will examine how human behavior is focused on the attainment of life goals, and go on to analyze how human diversity helps explain the multiple ways in which human needs can be met. Specific attention will be given to the concept of the dual perspective and to the ways in which ethnocentrism and oppression serve to perpetuate obstacles to the fulfillment of human potential. The exhibit that concludes the chapter, "The Violent Streets of Luis Guzman," provides an opportunity to apply concepts of systems, human diversity, and goal-directed behavior to a specific situation.

SYSTEMS

Definitions and Perspective

The generalist practitioner, in order to effectively mediate the transactions between persons and environments, must understand the interlocking network of structured relationships in which people live. Conceptualized as systems, these networks can be visualized as a series of smaller units nestled inside progressively larger ones, ranging in size from the individual to the family, the small group, the organization, the community, the society, and the culture. A systems perspective, by providing a model that focuses on multiple levels of phenomena simultaneously, helps the practitioner view behavior in context and shows how these units of varying size and levels of complexity mutually influence each other.

Viewing behavioral components in interaction is a difficult task. Our tendency is to see the world in static and linear terms, a view that alternates between focusing on the individual and the environment rather than looking at both simultaneously. Linear thinking assumes direct cause-and-effect relationships. This thinking tends to oversimplify complex issues and thus intervention plans are consequently based on an oversimplified interpretation of a complex reality. Systems thinking, focusing on the *interaction* between individual and environmental forces, helps the profession abandon these linear approaches, because it presents the same phenomena in terms of the dynamic relationship between the components in interaction.

A **system** can be defined as a whole made up of mutually interdependent parts. A system is both a part and a whole, so that small systems, such as individuals, families, and small groups, respond to and influence larger and more complex systems, such as neighborhoods, communities, and economic and political structures. A neighborhood can be analyzed, for instance, as a whole or as a part of a larger whole—a city. The systems model helps us understand the reciprocal interaction between the component parts. Political and economic structures, for example, have an impact on the lives of people. People, in turn, directly and indirectly influence political and economic structures. Two specific examples will further explain what we mean by systems.

The Human Body as a System

The body is a biological system composed of highly complex and sophisticated chemicals that interact to create the organs and biological processes that make human life possible. The body, however, is dependent on obtaining certain substances from outside itself—air, water, and food, for example. In addition, bodily processes are vulnerable to other external forces, such as temperature and physical traumas (blows that break the skin or the bones, for example). Thus we must describe a unit (in this case the human body) in terms of its internal components (blood, bones, chemical reactions, and so forth) and its relationships with other external units (the physical world, non-human animal life, and other humans). The regulation of bodily fluids and body temperature further exemplifies the interaction between the mechanisms of the body and external environmental forces. Fluid evaporating from the body through perspiration must be replaced, as must the salt which is also lost through perspiration. Life itself is dependent upon the quality of the interaction between the physical body and external environmental forces.

The Family as a System

The family is a social system composed of people who interact with each other in certain ways. A systems perspective views the members of a family not as isolated units but as interacting members. The ways in which they interact are determined by cultural expectations (e.g., who should raise the children, who should be the wage earner), socially structured situations (e.g., whether the family belongs to the dominant group or a minority group), and the biological and psychological characteristics of the members themselves (such as physical handicaps or emotional needs). The family, then, like the human body, can be described internally, in terms of its components, and externally, in terms of its relationships with its environment. We might note at this point that the family as a unit is made up of other units—the individual members. These individuals can then be further subdivided into component parts, thus suggesting the complexity of levels of interactions that can result.

We can call each unit of analysis a system—in the above examples, the human body and the family are both systems. Internal components and processes within each system further define the essence of the system, as do the systems' vital relationships with other systems. Systems describe reality by describing the structure and processes internal to a system as well as those which link one system to another. These two aspects of the way systems help us describe and understand reality are especially important for understanding a phenomenon as complex as human behavior. Our example further points out how small units, here families, are nestled within larger, more complex units, such as social institutions.

Carrying the example of the family one step further, it is easy to see one of the primary characteristics of a system—that changing the relationship between the parts changes the reality of the whole. The family, as a whole, is qualitatively and quantitatively different that its component parts, or individual systems of behavior. Rearranging the component parts—as in divorce, or the removal of a family member for hospitalization, military service, or death—dramatically affects the whole.

CHARACTERISTICS OF SYSTEMS

Systems theory is based on the assumption of the interconnectedness of all phenomena, including human behavior. Exerting pressure (action) on one part of the system effects a response (reaction) in another component of the system. Change occurring at the individual or family level, therefore, affects the neighborhood and the community. Political and economic changes in turn affect smaller units of social organization, such as the individual and the family. Human behavior, according to this perpective, is not only shaped by, but also shapes the environment in which it occurs. Systems theory offers the practitioner the analytical tools to conceptualize this chain of person-environment relationships in terms of their dynamic interplay. Exhibit 5.2 at the end of Chapter 5, from *American hunger crisis,* and the exhibit at the end of this chapter, are both taken from actual life experiences and serve as excellent case studies to illustrate the reciprocal effects of person-environment transactions.

We will now focus on four characteristics shared by systems of all sizes: boundaries, purpose, exchange, and network.

Boundaries

A system is an organized collection of activities and resources that exists within definable social and physical **boundaries** (Federico, 1984). The human person, for example, exists within the physically defined body, while the community has both physical (geographical) and social (who interacts with whom) boundaries.

Boundaries regulate the amount of energy (information, re-sources) exchanged between a system and its environment. An open system allows a constant interchange in which energy, information, and resources flow freely between a system and its environment. Closed systems allow no such exchange. Optimum functioning of a system requires that boundaries remain fluid and flexible. The boundaries of a given system need to be open enough to respond to changing environmental conditions—to incorporate new energy and information—yet be firm enough to maintain the internal integrity of the system. In assessing the health needs of a community, for instance, the health planner must consider the internal and external pressures (economic constraints, political reactions) that could make the boundaries more rigid if not properly handled. Family therapists similarly strive to maintain fluid communication patterns among the individual members of the family, thereby enhancing the energy interchange across boundaries.

Differentiating a system from its environment is an important part of the assessment phase of social intervention, and the concept of boundaries helps in accomplishing this task. A system, together with its environment, forms the total context for intervention. Careful demarcation of **subsystems** (the compo-nents of a system) helps the professional focus attention on manageable indicators, and narrows the field for consideration of potential influences on the system or subsystems. A hospital's social service unit, for instance, may be analyzed as its own system made up of its own components, such as personnel, services, and users of these services. These form subsystems within the unit. However, the whole social service unit may itself be part of the subsystem of a larger **suprasystem** which is a hospital organization. The hospital organization in turn becomes part of the larger health care system. The language of systems helps clarify the relationship between the boundaries of a system and its component parts, and the relationship between the parts themselves. In the case of the hospital social service unit, one might find that tension and stress between the supervisory staff and the direct service workers in the social service unit—that is, between parts of the system—negatively affect the ability of the social service department to work cooperatively with the nursing division—that is, the relationship between the system and part of its environment. These conflicts, in turn, directly and indirectly have an impact on the quality of service to individual clients.

The concept of boundaries can be readily extrapolated to apply to the biological, psychological, social-structural contexts. The biological structures of cell, organ, organ system, and organism, for example, while interdependent in function, can be isolated as separate entities for independent analysis by simple demarcation of boundaries such as skin, tissue, and membrane. Shifting the unit of attention from biological to psychological dimensions enables one to draw boundaries focusing on discrete personality traits or on the total personality system. Social-structural boundaries can be used to delimit family, political, and economic structures as well as to identify group, organization, and community variables. Religious, ideational, and value factors create cultural boundaries. The elaborate mechanisms employed to protect these boundaries range from psychological defensiveness to the intersocietal conflict seen in war.

Purpose

Survival is one of the primary purposes of most systems. In order for a system to achieve its goals, balance must be maintained among the components of the system and with the environmental forces interacting with it. The concept of **homeostasis** refers to the property of systems that maintains continued stability among the various system components. It refers to the regulatory processes through which the system achieves a state of internal and external balance, or equilibrium. Critics of the concept of homeostasis argue that it is essentially a conservative concept through which maintenance of the status quo becomes the primary motivating force of the system. Perpetuation of archaic welfare policies, for example, assures the continuation of the welfare bureaucracy while demonstrating little concern for the well-being of the consumer. The current trend in both private and public agencies of maintaining a balanced budget may be at the expense of the recipients of service. Equilibrium is maintained, but it can hardly be described as a desired state.

A view of purpose that directs the system to seek change and new experience as well as stability is compatible with practice as presented in this text. It is also consistent with the concept of an open system with fluid and flexible boundaries. Purpose is dramatically evidenced at the biological level in the infinite adaptive arrangements through which the continuation of the species is promoted. The progressive increase in complexity seen in biological systems illustrates the organism's simultaneous concern for survival and change. Maintaining the integrity of a system is, in and of itself, not enough. Growth and evolution of new and emerging forms is also a characteristic of life.

Social-structural explanations of behavior focusing on homeostasis have been targets of criticism by conflict theorists. Meninger (1963), for example, says the following:

> It would be one-sided indeed to ignore the fact that there are other determinants of human behavior than merely passive adjustment to it. There is a strong urge within the organism to effect change, to initiate some of the very disturbances which the regulatory processes of the organism are patterned to resist. It is the conflict between the wish for change—newness, variety, opportunity— and the fear of other consequences of change which makes for the complexity of human behavior.

The point of contention is that homeostasis implies that preservation of the status quo is the system's primary purpose. Uncritical application of biological concepts to social-structural phenomena, such as in the Social Darwinism of the nineteenth century or in some of the more recent developments in sociobiology, has profound implications for the welfare of humankind. It leaves the door open for "scientific" support of political ideologies and policies. Most social-structural theories, however, incorporate growth and change as part of a social system's management of internal and external forces. These are compatible with the goals of generalist practice.

Attitudes, ideas, and values related to such fundamental human concerns as family life, sex role identification, the meaning of work, and the existence (or nonexistence) of a deity form the nucleus around which cultural purposes are organized. A shared sense of purpose solidifies cultural boundaries, and much human effort is expended toward both maintaining and changing cultural goals. Having looked at purpose as one of the variables around which a system organizes its energy and draws its boundaries, we will now focus on two additional and related characteristics of systems: exchange and networks.

Exchange

The boundaries of a system, which establish the system's integrity, are usually permeable—that is, they are open to new sources of energy and information from the environment. The term **exchange** refers to the process of interaction between the system and its environment. Living systems require resources in order to function effectively and achieve their purposes. Resouces may be supplied from within the system or from the external environment. These internal or external resources may be thought of as **inputs;** once processed by the system, they result in **outputs.** The biological process of eating clearly illustrates this point: the body processes food (input) and discharges waste (output). Inputs can be real or imagined. If the individual interprets a situation as real (i.e., accepts it as input), it will produce real behavioral consequences (output). At times this may be a sort of circular trap—as can be seen in the situation known as the **self-fulfilling prophecy,** in which the individual behaves in a way that assures consequences consistent with his/her inter-pretation of a situation or event. An adolescent, for instance, may feel overly concious of bodily weight when in fact he/she falls well within the average weight range for his/her age group. The belief that "Nobody likes me 'cause I'm fat" results in defensive behavior which prevents him/her from making friends. Here the cultural values regarding desirable appearance (input) have been inter-preted and internalized, and are manifest in the individual's body image and social unease (output).

Social-structural exchanges can be conceptualized in terms of the reciprocal relationships occuring between individual (or family) systems and political, economic, and ideological systems.

For example, members of the nuclear family contribute labor (input) to the economic system in exchange for wages (output), and the nuclear family adheres to community standards (input) in exchange for acceptance (output) by the community.

Examination of the exchanges between and across system boundaries aids the professional in developing a dynamic interpretation of events and phenomena. It helps one understand, for instance, the interchanges between political and economic systems, as well as the relationships among family members. A government planning agency, for example, may be interested in assessing the impact of a proposed navy base installation on the economic life of the surrounding community. A worker studying the same phenomena in another setting may focus on the effect such development will have on community housing patterns. Such political and economic decisions have an impact on internal family dynamics like division of labor and patterns of leadership and authority. In the first case, political and economic systems become part of the environment of the family system. In the second case, the family is viewed as a part of the subsystem of larger political and economic systems.

Networks

Networks have been described as aggregations of connecting lines, links, or channels (Hanchett, 1979). These result from the system-environment exchanges discussed previously. A network may be a system in itself. The social welfare system, for instance, is a network of interrelated agencies and services; kinship systems are networks of related roles and relationships. A network, then, is established when a system of patterned relationships develops.

Any given system obtains input from other systems. Thus, inputs for one system are outputs for other systems. To look at a concrete example, the family system is dependent on input in the form of economic resouces (output from the economic system) and in the form of educational services (output from the public education system). The family processes these inputs to produce a number of its own outputs. Among them are such things as food and housing for its members, and youngsters properly nourished, motivated, and intellectually prepared to attend school. These outputs of the family system then become inputs to individual family members, who are biological systems. The family outputs also become inputs to the economic and educational systems. Any output has an impact, or an effect, on the system that uses it as an input. To continue the above example, if children are not adequately nourished, their growth and behavior will be seriously affected. In addition, children who are not prepared for school by the family pose a task for the educational system that is altogether different than if the children are prepared.

We can see, then, that the input, output, and impact experiences of each system become enmeshed in networks of interdependence that relate to the input, output, and impact of other systems. In other words, within the supersystem are networks of systems that impact on each other through the exchange of inputs and outputs. This is why behavior cannot be looked at out of context. It exists as part of a system which is, in turn, part of a network of systems. To adequately understand behavior, one has to place it within this larger context. The social problems of racism, sexism, ageism, and homophobia (fear of homosexuals) serve as examples. They are deeply rooted cultural components that affect the social-structural arrangements through which goods and services are allocated. For instance, forcing the elderly out of the work force condemns many of them to poverty and accelerated physical and mental deterioration through the interaction of the economic, political, and family systems. Such complex problems are created and perpetuated through system networks and cry for systemic rather than individual resolution. Those offering professional help need to be aware of these networks in order to select appropriate kinds of intervention.

Understanding the concept of systems will help you, as a generalist practitioner, put isolated components of human behavior into an integrated whole. It is important, however, to remember that just as systems share many characteristics, any given system is made up of a unique set of people with unique boundaries, purposes, exchanges, and networks. We will shift our focus now to purpose and motivation and then to the concept of human diversity and develop a perspective that will help you understand its role in determining behavior.

PURPOSE AND MOTIVATION

People do not generally act randomly. Most of their behavior is directed toward the attainment of a **purpose,** in other words, a goal or a desired event. The goals people seek may be biological, psychological, social, or cultural, and they may be individual or group-oriented. People eat to maintain their bodily functions—a biological goal. They cry to express or release emotion—a psychological goal. They go to work to earn money in order to have the things they want—a combination of social goals (working to get money) and psychological or even biological goals (the satisfaction of having what one wants, some of which is necessary for survival). The fact that some people go to work in a factory and others labor at the edge of fishing holes cut in the Arctic ice reflects cultural values and material technology. People do not just act independently, nor do they seek only to attain their own purposes. Many of the systems discussed earlier in the chapter organize people to act together in order to attain large-scale group goals. Soldiers fight in units so that their nation will win, thereby preserving their way of life. The citizens of nations vote in order to ensure orderly decision making and social control for the society as a whole.

Human purpose, then, serves as a source of **motivation**, meaning that purpose stimulates behavior or action. People's goals lead them to engage in **goal-directed behavior**—activities that will attain those goals. Many of these activities are routinized through social norms and social institutions. For example, we know that if we are to keep our jobs we have to get up in the morning and arrive at work on time. Because our jobs allow us to fulfill many goals for ourselves, as noted above, we are motivated to do what we must to keep them. Because most workers seek their goal (keeping their job) by acting predictably, corporations and other businesses can also achieve their goals (providing services, making profits, and so on).

Strategies for attaining other types of goals are less clear-cut. We need to feel loved and accepted, yet sometimes we are not sure how to accomplish this. The goal is important, so we try various things to achieve it—we might smile a lot, do nice things for other people, try to excel at whatever we do, not lose our temper, and so forth. Most people do things that have a reasonable probability of getting them what they want most of the time. However, some people do things that seem self-defeating. For example, in an effort to find acceptance, many young people succumb to social pressure to use drugs or alcohol. Whether or not these activities lead to acceptance by their peers, they are likely to lead to other kinds of problems that can interfere with the attainment of other goals. For example, being addicted to drugs is related to physical problems, losing jobs, crime, and arrest.

This is where understanding the link between purpose and behavior can seem weak. It may seem odd that people are acting purposefully when what they are actually doing is hurting themselves. Yet as the example above shows, this can be the case. Trying to attain one goal sometimes leads to behavior that interferes with others. It would be a mistake to assume that people were acting randomly just because what they were doing was, at least in part, self-defeating. A holistic view is important, as you already know. Once we understand all of the goals that are being sought, we can figure out what behaviors are tied to what goal-seeking efforts. It is then easier to help people learn need-meeting strategies that are more likely to enable them to attain all their goals with minimal adverse effects.

COMMON HUMAN NEEDS

All systems seek to meet their needs by acting in purposeful ways. At any system level, some of these needs are shared by all, while others are unique to particular groups. For example, at the level of individuals as biological systems, adequate nutrition is a **common human need,** one shared by all human beings and one that is basic to survival. Other levels of systems also have common needs. Bureaucracies have to develop system maintenance procedures that make possible the effective organization of their workers and the attainment of production goals. Families and other small groups require enough group cohesion for members to want to remain. Communities need sufficient cooperation and interdependence to ensure workable governance procedures.

Towle (1965) and Maslow (1970) are best known for their formulation of common human needs at the level of individuals as systems. Maslow lists physiological needs (such as condition of the blood, the body's chemical balance, sensory perception, and hormonal functioning), safety needs (security, stability, freedom from fear and anxiety, need for structure, and others), belong-ingness and love needs (affection, feeling "rooted," feeling accepted, and so on), esteem needs (self-respect, self-esteem, a sense of mastery, a sound reputation, and so forth), and the need for self-actualization, or "becoming everything that one is capable of becoming" (Maslow, 1970, pp. 35-46). (Towle, 1965, pp. 6-11) offers a similar formulation: she lists physical welfare, personality development, emotional growth, development of intellectual capacity, relationships with others, and spiritual needs.

Because people have common human needs, they create or structure environments to help them meet those needs. The earth itself is part of this, as we grow food in the soil and utilize water for drinking, for power, and for movement. Of course much of the environment is social, having been created by society and culture. Social decisions about ways to meet common human needs interact with biological and other natural factors. Whereas early peoples lived in shelters made from skins or mud, today we find shelter (a common human need) in many types of structures reflecting a wide range of technology. Nutrition is available through the use of artificial products, and opportunities to establish reputations and "self-actualize" are frequently found in large-scale bureaucracies. Meeting needs for affection and a sense of well-being and belonging occurs in a wide range of social groupings, ranging from traditional families through bowling clubs to groups concerned with ethnic and racial identity.

The idea of common human needs serves to link knowledge of systems and goal-directed behavior. Each type of system has its own particular basic needs that must be met if it is to survive. This provides a powerful stimulus for action. Because some systems are individual and others are composed of many people, some actions will be individual and others will be collective. Remember, too, the idea of systems-within-systems (subsystems and supra-systems). The residents of a community comprise a community system, but each is also an individual system. Some of their behavior will focus on meeting individual system needs, and others on meeting the needs of the larger system. The more we understand the characteristics of each particular system, the more we can identify system goals and behavior oriented toward the attainment of those goals. In addition, understanding that systems have exchanges with each other, and that they develop systemic networks helps us to see how goal-attainment efforts of individual systems have an impact on, or are affected by, similar behaviors in other systems.

HUMAN DIVERSITY

Although systems of the same type share common needs, the ways in which these needs are met may vary considerably. Some large bureaucracies seek to motivate their workers with profit-sharing plans, while others provide benefits such as swimming pools, free parking, and low-cost meals in a company cafeteria. Some families express love through a great deal of physical touching, while others do so by the provision of elaborate material resources such as clothes and cars. And, of course, some people meet their nutritional needs with steak, others with fried bananas, and still others with raw fish. The needs at each system level are common, but the strategies for meeting them are quite different.

When we look at these differences we are not evaluating one as better or worse than another, for to do so would be to adopt an ethnocentric point of view. The reason that we do not want to adopt this viewpoint is **human diversity.** This refers to the biological, psychological, social-structural, and cultural ways in which people are different. Chapters 1 and 2 discussed reasons why these differences exist. The genetic inheritance of people makes them different, with some being tall and others short, some women and others men, some black and others Oriental, some young and others old, and so on. As people grow (biological) and have life experiences (social and cultural), their psychological characteristics emerge. People become characterized by high or low intelligence, calm or agitated personalities, and cooperative or competitive spirits. They then bring their biological and psychological characteristics into their social world, making friends easily or with difficulty, working steadily or moving from job to job, getting married or choosing to remain single.

The sources of human diversity, then, are biological, psychological, social-structural, and cultural. People bring with them their own particular characteristics and life histories. These interact with the needs and characteristics of the systems in which they function. Sometimes this interaction occurs smoothly, but many times it does not. In order to understand this process, a **dual perspective** is helpful. This suggests that all behavior is viewed in two ways. The first is how people see their own behavior, and the second is how outsiders view that same behavior (Norton, 1978, pp. 3-12). Members of a particular system assess their behavior in terms of the standards learned in that system. A secretary at IBM is taught to be polite but impersonal when answering business phone calls. A customer with whom she is speaking may feel frustrated by this very same impersonality if he/she has learned that interactions should be more personal. In order to understand what happens as these two systems interact, we must be able to see both points of view.

THE EXPERIENCE OF DIVERSITY

The dual perspective allows us to see that people are constantly managing two parts of themselves. As people, they develop a sense of identity. Biologically they learn that they are "pretty," "sexy," or "a brain." Psychologically they come to understand themselves as warm and loving, aggressive and controlling, placid or hot-headed. They also attach themselves to various kinds of ethnic, racial, and socioeconomic group identities. Lower paid workers soon see that they are different from the wealthy Fifth Avenue residents whose groceries they deliver. Not only are they different, they also come to see themselves as members of a lower social class. Even larger systems develop identities. The city of Tuscon has developed community pride around its efforts to do minimal damage to its desert ecology, and many large Japanese corporations perceive themselves as very concerned about the well-being of their workers.

These identities become important in two ways. They strongly influence the goals that people (and larger systems) consider appropriate and attainable. When self-identity is positive, it tends to encourage people to take command over their own lives. When it is negative, the effect is often to make people doubt their ability to function effectively. Members of minority groups are frequently victimized by negative self-identities. Aaron Fricke's account of growing up as a gay man is a good example (Fricke, 1981). He describes how, after a childhood that included spontaneous and highly enjoyable sexual encounters with other boys, he became labeled as a "queer" in adolescence. Although his behavior had not changed at all, others' responses to it had. As a result, he changed from a happy child to a troubled and very unhappy teenager. It was only when he started to make contact with other gay men, who were able to reinforce his sense of himself as a decent person, that he was able to emerge as an adult with a secure sense of self. During the period when his self-identity was being attacked, however, he withdrew from his former activities and became very isolated. This is quite common for people who believe that they are worthless.

The other way in which identity is important is the effect that it has on members of other groups. The dual perspective alerts us to the fact that people are constantly reacting to the behavior of members of groups of which they are *not* a part. In other words, some portion of their own identity is formed in relation to those other groups. For example, some men who believe that women are too "emotional" reinforce their own sense of identity as "strong" by comparing themselves with women. Unfortunately, this can often lead to oppressive behavior by those who consider themselves superior to members of other groups. Identity, then, develops in each system in part through its interaction with other systems. Once formed, it tends to influence the kinds of behavior in which people engage.

Among the most dramatic aspects of human existence have been the incidences of identity reformulation that have occured through history. Our own time has had several examples. The Civil Rights movement of the 1950s and 1960s dramatically changed the self-perception of many black people who had previously doubted their abilities and self-worth. "Black is beautiful" became a rallying cry for black people to assert their competence to participate fully in society. As a result, blacks began to have at least limited access to social systems that had been closed to them for centuries. The women's and the gay/lesbian liberation movements of the 1970s and 1980s have had similar effects for these groups. The elderly and the physically disabled have also had recent successes in redefining their identities. These historical events demonstrate the importance of self-identity for social participation. They also illustrate how identity is an interactional process between those seeking an identity and those who are reacting to it.

THE CONSEQUENCES OF HUMAN DIVERSITY

The fact that people meet their common needs in different ways—the phenomenon of human diversity—has two very significant effects on people's lives. It affects their **life styles,** the choices made about how to carry out life tasks. It also affects their **life chances,** or access to basic life-sustaining and life-enriching resources. Life styles are the most visible means for distinguishing between different systems. These include such things as styles of clothing, whether members of families eat their meals together, organizational policies, and community architecture. Life style reflects a group or person's identity, and is often a blend of those things a group defines as important along with some of the views of outsiders. For example, Italian-American families may incorporate both traditional Italian beliefs that the man is the head of the house and American values which allow women more freedom than strict paternalistic cultures.

In general, life style is of concern to helping professionals in two ways. The more common is that it must be understood if the helper is going to be able to interact effectively with members of diverse groups. Knowing, for example, that ministers frequently have considerable power in black communities helps those who work in these communities. But life style is also of concern because of its visibility to society at large. The image that people have of groups is heavily influenced by what they see and experience. Notice that large corporations go to considerable length to create impressive corporate headquarters. This projects a public image of solidity and competence. On the other hand,

Anglos who hear loud dance music while walking through a *barrio* in Los Angeles may assume that Chicanos are fun-loving but irresponsible.

In this way, life style may lead to the stereotyping of members of particular systems. This, then, becomes the basis for restricting life chances through oppression. If you think for a moment about the biological, psychological, social-structural, and cultural sources of diversity, you will realize that any group is characterized by both similarity and difference. Members of the group share the characteristics that define membership in that group. For example, women share a gender, Puerto Ricans an ethnicity, the elderly a chronical age, and the handicapped a physical limitation. However, within each group there is also considerable diversity. Women vary in terms of race, ethnicity, and age, Puerto Ricans may be of any age and race, the elderly of any socioeconomic and educational level, and the handicapped of any sex and ethnicity. Therefore, whenever stereotypes are developed about a group they will inevitably be inaccurate because of the variations within the group. As a result, many people will be treated in very inappropriate ways.

The key is the inappropriate treatment of people. Any system that stereotypes people and groups, especially for the purpose of disadvantaging them, treats people as *categories* rather than as *individuals.* However, categorizing people creates distance from them. This is often captured by a label that serves to focus attention on perceptions that are negative and dehumanizing. Terms like "queer," "nigger," "wop," and "bitch" are all used to devalue people in a very impersonal, dehumanized way. They are no longer people with hopes, needs, and self-worth. Therefore, it no longer matters how they are treated because they have been defined as unimportant and faceless.

The result of stereotyping and labeling is **oppression,** the systematic restriction of people's life chances based on institutionalized prejudice and discrimination. In terms of access to all the major categories of life-sustaining and life-enriching resources, members of oppressed groups are disadvantaged. Not only is poverty growing, but it is also very unequally distributed, with families headed by single-parent women, blacks, and Hispanics most at risk (Pear, 1983). A recent study of the homeless in

Phoenix showed members of minority groups, the severely mentally disabled, chronic substance abusers, and the physically handicapped most affected (Stark, 1984). Women and blacks continue to be paid less than men and whites (*The New York Times*, 1984), a fact that is correlated to the poverty noted above. Low income correlates with high rates of malnutrition and infant mortality (Stewart, 1984). The reality of these figures can be seen daily in slums populated by minority group members who live in substandard housing, go to inadequate schools, endure crime as a part of daily life, are excluded from employment, and are tempted to escape through alcohol or drugs.

Oppression is not an intellectual concept. It describes day-to-day life that offers illness, danger, discomfort, and hopelessness. It is not something that just happens, either. It is the result of social-structural arrangements that systematically create an **underclass,** a group of people who are excluded from the mainstream of America's social institutions (Auletta, 1982). And oppression happens because of human diversity in conjunction with ethnocentrism. People are different from each other. Rather than viewing these differences as resources rich with opportunities for societal development, they are used to categorize and disadvantage people. Efforts of majority groups to oppress minority groups set the stage for conflict. As noted above, some groups have entered into the struggle to improve their collective position. Many have been successful in terms of a more positive self-identity and greater (but still limited) access to basic resources. But as long as oppression continues, further conflict is an ever-present probability.

When understanding oppression we also should look beyond basic life-sustaining resources. Maslow (1970), when talking about self-actualization, talked about people becoming all that they could be. He was, in effect, talking about the quality of life, not just survival. Oppression makes even survival problematic, but the whole idea of human diversity as both natural and a potential resource goes far beyond mere survival. Underlying the idea of cultural pluralism is the idea that different groups have distinctive contributions to make to the whole of society. In other words, they have resources. Oppression blocks these resources, turning them instead into obstacles for members of oppressed groups. Waste is always costly. This is true at the societal level just as much as at the personal level. In a world of increasing scarcity, the question must be raised whether our planet can continue to waste the resources that diverse groups offer to the human enterprise.

THE COMMITMENT OF PROFESSIONAL HELPERS

To conclude this section on human diversity, as well as the chapter, a brief look at the role of professional helpers in societal change will be useful. In Chapter 1 the purpose of professional helping was defined as helping people to function more effectively by facilitating transactions between them and their environments. The systems perspective enables us to see how people function as systems within larger systems. A simultaneous focus on all these system levels shows how they mutually influence each other. Part of the functioning of each system is the diverse human characteristics that effect the exchanges between systems, blocking the ability of systems to share resources and creating artificial obstacles.

This suggests that many person-environment transactions become problematic because of problems in the environment (e.g., larger systems). When ethnocentrism, prejudice, stereotyping, labeling, discrimination, and oppression occur, the best way for the professional helper to improve person-environment transactions is to work toward change in the environment. To be sure, environmental conditions such as oppression have effects on individuals. People become depressed, act out, drop out, and get sick. These problems have to be addressed so that the person as a biopsychosocial system can be healed and function more effectively. However, until the environmental systems that deprive people of the life-sustaining and life-enriching resources that they need are changed, individuals are likely to continue to struggle and sometimes break down (Brown, 1984).

Societal change is never easy, and only results from sustained and organized effort by many people. Diverse groups offer a strategy for working toward such change, however. All systems have resources that are distinctive. These are sometimes called natural helping systems, and are often most visible in the form of self-help groups. The systems and groups operate at all system levels. Individuals can choose to control their own health by managing diet and stress more effectively. People with eating problems band together through groups like Weight Watchers and Overeaters Anonymous. Members of professions form professional associations, workers form unions, community residents form community councils, members of racial and ethnic groups form groups to advocate their interests, and so on. These organized expressions of a group's view of itself and its goals have within them the power to work toward these goals. By helping these groups to organize and function effectively, professional helpers will be emphasizing the strength inherent in diversity, and increasing opportunities to reduce ethnocentrism and oppression. This, in turn, supports the attainment of the purposes of professional helping.

SUMMARY

This chapter has extended the concept of a holistic view of human behavior. We have seen that behavior is organized into systems which exist at many levels, ranging from individual to societal and cultural systems. Each system is concerned with attaining purposes, some of which are shared by all similar systems and others of which are unique to particular systems. The way purposes and goals are sought reflects the human diversity characteristics of systems. Interaction between systems sometimes leads to oppression, in which the life chances of members of some systems are methodically restricted by other systems. Oppression is supported by cultural ethnocentric beliefs and social-structural arrangements that result from them, and it can only be changed by intervention at these levels. However, people's daily lives are affected by oppression, and help at the individual and small-group levels is as needed as change efforts focused on larger systems. Focusing on both levels is necessitated by the commitment of helping professionals to improve the transactions between people and their environments.

STUDY QUESTIONS

1. According to the systems approach, change introduced in one part of the system effects change in other parts of the system. What is the implication of this for the social welfare professional's task of directing change at the individual level? At the family level? At the community level?

2. Systems theory, or selected ideas and concepts implicit in it, can easily be represented graphically. Make a diagram in which your class is viewed as a social system—illustrate its boundaries, then chart its relationship to the various suprasystems of which it is a part and the subsystems that constitute its components.

3. Societal resources are allocated through social-structural arrangements encompassing political, economic, and ideational systems. How does the interrelationship of these systems impact on the public social policy of income maintenance? Health care? The role and status of women and minorities?

4. Professionals need to keep in mind that there is a great deal of diversity within any ethnic group. What are some of the variables that account for variations within groups?

5. All of us have strong feelings about certain diverse groups. Some find it difficult to accept the elderly, others the physically handicapped, or homosexuals. What groups do you have difficulty accepting even though you may understand them intellectually? What is the basis of your feelings? To what extent do these feelings affect your behavior?

6. One perceives life goals based on the alternatives provided by the culture in which one lives. What alternatives does contemporary American culture provide for women in terms of career choices? How do these differ from options available for men? How do they differ from the alternatives available to women twenty-five years ago?

7. Discuss Exhibit 3.1, "The Violent Streets of Luis Guzman," from a systems perspective, from the perspective of human diversity, and in terms of goal-directed behavior.

KEY TERMS

Boundary That which separates a system from its environment. The identifiable limits of a system.

Common human need A need shared by all human beings and which is basic for survival.

Dual perspective Understanding the self-view of a population, as well as the view of other groups that evaluate its behavior.

Exchange The process of interaction between a system and its environment.

Goal-directed behavior Behavior that is directed toward achievement and is accomplished through the problem-solving process.

Homeostasis The tendency of a system to maintain a relatively stable equilibrium among its various components.

Human diversity Differences between individuals and groups based on biological, cultural, social, and psychological variables.

Input Internal or external resources for a system.

Life chances Access to basic life-sustaining and life-enriching resources.

Life style Choices about how to carry out life tasks.

Motivation Something that stimulates behavior or action.

Network Aggregations of connecting lines, links, or channels among systems.

Oppression Systematic restriction of people's life chances based on institutional prejudice and discrimination.

Output Resources that have been processed by a system and transformed into a system product.

Purpose A goal or desired event.

Self-fulfilling prophecy Action that assures consequences that will confirm interpretation of a situation or event by an individual or group.

Subsystem A component of a larger system.

Suprasystem A larger system that incorporates smaller ones.

System A whole composed of interrelated and interdependent parts.

Underclass People who are excluded from the mainstream of the dominant culture's social institutions.

Exhibit 3.1, "The Violent Streets of Luis Guzman," recounts the family, school, peer, and crime experiences of a young Puerto Rican man in New York City. As you read about his life, focus on the systems in which he functions. What are their purposes and goals, and what strategies do they use to attain them? You will see how Luis is a small, individual system within larger, more complex systems. You will also begin to understand how the goals of many systems were to some degree incompatible with Luis's goals for himself. As a result, exchanges became blocked and distorted. The particular human diversity characteristics of Luis and his family were also significant. Family tensions reflected cultural values, sexism, and poverty. Problems with other systems, such as the schools, the work place, and the criminal justice system, also had roots in cultural differences as well as Luis's age, gender, and psychological characteristics. Disentangling the system networks involved in Luis's situation poses a formidable challenge for helping professionals. It is clear that such an effort would require intervention in both small and large systems.

3.1: The Violent Streets of Luis Guzman

Avenue D on the Lower East Side of Manhattan is only 12 blocks long. But it is one of the meanest streets in America, a narrow corridor of poverty and violence running north from Houston Street, parallel to the East River and just across town from the leafy tranquillity of Greenwich Village.

It is a street where murders take place in the afternoon sunlight, where drug dealers operate boldly, fearing one another more than the police who occasionally cruise past in radio cars; a street where men gripping beer bottles in brown paper bags exchange prison memories, while little boys practice kung fu and karate and their mothers shop with food stamps for Cafe Bustelo and yellow rice.

It is a street of housing projects and crumbling tenements, some abandoned and burned out, a street where the language of choice is Spanish and the old men play dominoes.

For Luis Guzman, the third of six children born to an illiterate, heavy-drinking delivery

continued

truck driver and a chronically ill, listless mother, Avenue D was the center of the world.

It was the guerrilla base where he "hung out"as a member of the "Little Wild Boys" gang, where he bought his first gun, a .32-caliber revolver, for $75, and where he and his friends planned raids into the Upper East Side to mug and snatch gold chains. It was where he headed first after he got out of Rikers Island and other institutions.

Luis Guzman is one of tens of thousands of violent youths who prowl the streets of the nation's cities, instilling fear and limiting in countless ways the manner in which urban Americans live their lives.

By this fall, at the age of 16, Luis Guzman had become a familiar figure to the police. He was arrested in September on charges of stealing a teacher's purse at a public school. His history made him a natural suspect for the police in the slaying later that month of a 38-year-old lawyer in a robbery in a riverside park near Avenue D, and he spent two weeks in jail before three other youths were arrested in the crime.

Before the murder charge was dropped, the authorities discovered that eight months earlier Luis had violated probation for an armed-robbery conviction by running away from a sort of halfway house for juvenile delinquents in East Harlem. So, for now, he remains in custody at Rikers Island.

Like many other young criminals, Luis has spent much of his life in institutions, where he has had hundreds of hours of group therapy and counseling. He has repeatedly run away.

Specialists in the field offer little hope of reversing the trend of growing violence by young people. Some say a complete overhaul of all the social services, including the schools, is needed. Three years ago, New York State stiffened its penalties for 13-, 14-, and 15-years-olds convicted of such major crimes as armed robbery, rape and murder. But sometimes, major offenses are still referred to the Family Court, where most juvenile crimes are handled and where the maximum penalty is no more than 18 months of confinement.

Such things never concerned Luis when he was carrying out a mugging. He was never anxious, never afraid, he said the other day in a bare visiting room at Rikers Island.

"I don't be thinking," he said. "My mind go blank."

Like many other young criminals, Luis grew up in a family with little structure. The family moved from one dilapidated tenement to another. Neither parent paid much attention to the children. Meals and bedtimes could come at any time. Sometimes there was no food at all in the house. Once,

continued

one of Luis's sisters was bitten by a rat as she slept.

Luis's earliest memory is of cutting classes. By the age of 8 he was working as a lookout for shoplifters. He moved on to shoplifting, tried burglary, snatched gold chains, mugged and held up a jewelry store, he says.

Stealing is the only kind of work Luis has ever done. He never worried about the terror he inflicted on his victims, or about their physical loss. His only concern was that he might have the bad luck to attack someone armed with a gun, or that he might be caught.

Didn't Worry About Victims

Luis's parents, Felix and Haydee Guzman, say all of their children have been difficult, but that Luis has been more so than the rest. Except for 17-year-old Felix Guzman Jr., who spent time on Rikers Island for burglary, none of the others have been in jail.

Luis, his parents said, would not obey them. He fought constantly with his brothers, broke windows in the apartment buildings where the family lived and stole from members of the family: $140 and some food stamps from his mother, an inexpensive watch from his father, a $500 radio from the woman with whom his father now lives.

"He thought nobody loved him," his father said.

Keeping track of Luis was beyond either parent. Neither remembers what schools the boy attended. They remember some, but not all, of the institutions he has lived in, beginning with a brief stay in a Roman Catholic home when he was 5 years old and his mother told the authorities that she was incapable of taking care of him and some of the other children. The arrests and his escapes are a jumble in their minds.

Counselors, teachers and criminal-justice officials remember Luis as a hypertensive child who went into special classes because he could not keep up with the others his age in school; who sometimes looked like a model youth while inside an institution, but who unfailingly got into trouble on the street.

Luis Guzman is slender and small, no more than 5 feet 6 inches tall. He wears his dark hair in a crew cut and looks out at the world through black coral eyes, his jaw set in a mask of repose. His speech is slow and direct.

That afternoon at Rikers Island, Luis described his feelings after a mugging. He would think: " 'Damn, I bet they be telling the cops right now.' I be getting nervous. The cops got my picture, and I be getting nervous that I going to be busted."

continued

What is wrong with robbing, Luis said, is that "you could run into the wrong person. He could turn around and shoot you. That's what I was afraid of. But I still done it anyway. I took big risks for the money. I like to support myself. I do it to support myself, that's why."

As for the victims, Luis said: "We'd just say, 'We got over. We took the money without getting busted.' I don't be thinking about them. I just think of getting the money and hanging out."

Sometimes Luis mugged with his bare hands, sometimes with a knife with a six-inch blade that he bought for $8.

'Run Up and Yoke 'Em'

"Sometimes you run up in the back and yoke 'em," with an arm around the neck. Luis said, "and the other boys take the money out of his pockets."

With a knife, he said, "You just put it in front of them and tell them, 'Give me your money.' We tell them to walk the opposite direction. Then we walk the other way. When we get to the corner we run."

Anyone who tried to rob him, Luis said, would have to kill him to get his money. If someone resisted him, he said, "I'd probably put them to sleep. My friend would yoke 'em." If he had a knife, he said, "I'll probably stick 'em."

" I don't stick 'em up here," he said, gesting toward the chest. "I'll probably stick 'em in the leg, down there."

Luis said he had stabbed only one person. That was his oldest brother, 18-year-old Ramiro, and it was an accident, he said. The day before Luis's latest arrest, he and Ramiro were fighting over who was going to wear one of Ramiro's shirts. Luis drew a kitchen knife. Ramiro threw a karate kick and hit the tip of the knife with his thigh. It was just enough to break the skin. Luis ran out the door, and Ramiro hurled a table at him. The next the family heard from Luis, more than 24 hours later, he had been picked up and charged with murder.

Felix and Haydee Guzman, who had come to New York from Puerto Rico as teen-agers, did not marry until 1965, after the birth of their fourth child, Evelyn.

Mrs. Guzman, now 39 years old, short and plump, speaks of an extremely jealous and violent husband. He forbade her to wear makeup, she said. He would come home late at night drunk, she said, and whistle for her to unlock the door.

"If I didn't open the door right away he would hit me," she said one afternoon in her sparely finished apartment in the Lillian Wald Houses on Avenue D, as blue flames flickered in the four burners on the cooking stove to provide warmth.

continued

Three years ago, Mrs. Guzman began attending services of the Pentacostal Church. Now she goes four or five times a week. This day she sat with her son Ramiro at a flimsy Formica-covered kitchen table, a bowl of plastic fruit in front of them, her hand resting on a Bible. In the small living room, with its bare tile floor, her daughter Haydee, 12, perched on a plaid, plastic-covered love seat, watching a movie on a black-and-white television set.

Would Stay Up Waiting

"If I took too long to open the door, he would think another man was in the house," Mrs. Guzman continued. "Sometimes I would stay up all night waiting for him to come home so he wouldn't get mad."

Her eyes glistened as she spoke of her husband, drunk and furious, shaking her like a child's doll, banging her head and shoulders against the wall. Ramiro, who was to join the Army in a few days, said his drunken father used to wake the children at 3 or 4 in the morning, line them up in the living room and whip them with an extension cord.

Felix Guzman, 49 years old, his face wrinkled and scarred, several front teeth missing, denies it all.

"I never hit her," he said. "I never touched my children."

Luis said that his father would slap his face when he lied or skipped school, but that he never beat him.

The woman with whom Mr. Guzman now lives on East 13th Street in a fifth-floor walkup crowded with appliances, knickknacks and bulky, faded furniture, said: "Me and him, we always argue. Sometimes he hits me and I hit him back." A rat bounded out of the kitchen garbage can and disappeared behind the washing machine with a clatter. The woman asked that her name not be published for fear that her welfare payments would be affected.

Felix Guzman has been in more than a few fights. Once, when he made the mistake of complaining that he was being cheated at cards, he was shot in the knee. Another time, while drinking in the storefront social club, he was stabbed in the back.

In the first months together, Felix and Haydee did not have an apartment of their own. Once, they were staying in the basement of a building where a friend worked as the superintendent. They slept on a couch. The temperature was 15 degrees. Haydee, who had been paralyzed by rheumatic fever for several months at age 11, suffered.

Over the years her health worsened. She would suffer with fever and swollen joints for

continued

months. Two years ago, she underwent surgery to replace one of the valves in her heart. She sees a doctor monthly at Beth Israel Medical Center.

Felix Guzman was not sympathetic.

"I'm working driving a truck," he said. "I come in and I find her in bed, 'Oh, my heart, my heart.' I come to eat and I have to go out to the store for it. I know she was not so sick she couldn't cook, that she can't do any job in the house. She didn't want to do anything."

In the fall of 1974, Haydee Guzman decided she could take no more. She left Felix.

Within two years he obtained a divorce decree giving him custody of the three eldest boys. He was not required to pay alimony or child support. Haydee Guzman went on welfare.

Not long after the Guzmans' separation, Mrs. Guzman recalled, her boys were found alone late at night at Felix's tenement on East 12th Street, playing on the fire escape in their underwear. Ramiro's jaw was swollen from an infected tooth.

Mrs. Guzman's mother telephoned the police, and they took Ramiro to the hospital.

Within a few days, Luis, Felix Jr. and Ramiro were living in a rambling, three-story Victorian home run by the Catholic Guardian Society on Staten Island. Luis was now 9.

There were 10 boys at the home, including the Guzmans, all with troubled backgrounds. Terry O'Neil, a slender, committed social worker with a master's degree, and his wife, Denise, who has a master's in educating children with special learning problems, were in charge.

"We treated them like our own children," Mr. O'Neil recalled. "The idea is to put them in a family structure, give them something to respect, get them to go to school."

At the home, everyone got out of bed at about 7 A.M. After breakfast there were assigned cleaning chores. Then it was off to school. After a recreation period and dinner, there were more chores and an hour of homework. At 8, the television went on for the first time in the day. By 9, the youngest of the children were being put to bed.

Mr. O'Neil remembers Luis warmly. "I liked Luis," he said. "I think he was a good kid. He liked sports, baseball and football. He was in the Cub Scouts. Luis wasn't a violent kid when I knew him. He wasn't even a street kid until he started running away."

Mr. O'Neil and some of the others who have worked with Luis believe frustration in school may have led him to become a runaway. No one seems to know for sure, not even Luis.

"I just wanted to be out in the world," he said at Rikers Island. "I wanted to travel to a lot

continued

of places, go to the Bronx and hang out."

In any case, the running, which began after Luis had been in the Catholic home for more than two years, seems to have been a turning point.

"He started meeting the wrong kind of kids," Mr. O'Neil said. "There's no one else to meet at 2 o'clock in the morning."

At Public School 20 on Staten Island, Luis had been diagnosed as having an unspecified mental impairment. He was placed in a special class with nine other pupils who were having difficulty learning to read and to solve elementary mathematics problems.

"Teachers would complain about his disruptive behavior in the classroom," said Mr. O'Neil. "Usually it was arguing with other students, more yelling, threatening. Fist fights. He wouldn't come home from school. He wouldn't get on the school bus."

Psychiatrists and other social workers were called in to talk with Luis. The Catholic Guardian Society thought he might settle down in another home. So he was transferred again.

One night around midnight, Luis and some other boys broke into Public School 20. "We took some cameras and film projectors," he said.

The police caught the boys and took them to the Spofford Juvenile Center, a gray fortress-like house of detention in the Bronx with heavy locked doors and surrounded by a 20-foot high wall. It was the first time Luis had been in a locked institution.

From Spofford, Luis was sent to another Catholic home on Staten Island. "I was there one day and I left," he said.

The Catholic Guardian Society told the Family Court, in effect, that they could not handle Luis. Eventually, the court ordered him to the Cardinal McClosky home in White Plains, N.Y., also an institution without locks.

"I never stayed for a long time, only four or five months," Luis said, "Then I left back to the city and stayed with my friend, this dude Markham."

Markham was a little older. He had his own apartment on Sixth Street near Avenue D. Luis sometimes called his friend "Mark," sometimes "Big Man."

By now, Luis was 14 years old. One day, Luis said, he and Mark were walking in Chinatown. It was sometime in 1979; Luis is not sure what month. He says he does not remember the name of the street. He had his .32, Mark was carrying a shotgun. Suddenly, he noticed that Mark was no longer at his side.

"I turned around and he wasn't there, so I walked back," Luis said. " I saw him holding up this jewelry store. He had his gun out, so I took mine out and I said,

continued

'This is a stickup.' The guy gave us jewelry. My boy knocked him out with his gun in his face.

"We went back to my mother's house, and they caught me there. I was sleeping. Somebody knocked on the door about 5 o'clock in the morning. One cop told my sister to open the door. Then they came and put guns in my face and told me: 'Don't move.' So I didn't move."

Luis says the police took him back to Spofford. He turned 15 there.

Luis's criminal records do not include the jewelry-store robbery he described. Either the information was lost or the case was dropped, authorities say, or Luis invented it. All, they say, are equally plausible possibilities in the realm of juvenile delinquency, where prosecution and record-keeping are uneven and where tales of self-aggrandizement are not rare.

The record does show, however, that Luis was accused of a robbery in Westchester County in the spring of 1979, apparently at the time he ran away from the Cardinal McClosky home. The charge was reduced to attempted grand larceny in the third degree, a misdemeanor rather than the original felony, and a Family Court judge ordered him sent to an institution run by the State Division for Youth, the agency charged with housing juvenile delinquents.

Luis passed a few more months in Spofford. Then in late January 1980, he went to the Great Valley Youth Camp in the densely wooded foothills of the Allegheny Mountains. The camp has no locked doors, barred windows or fences

Twice, shortly after he arrived, Luis ran away from Great Valley. But he was as lost in the countryside as a giraffe on Fifth Avenue. And he apparently decided to bide his time. There were 59 other boys at Great Valley: they ranged in age from 11 to 16. All but a handful had been arrested for major crimes such as robbery, rape and arson.

In the fall of 1980, Luis was allowed to go home for a visit of five days. He returned to Great Valley on schedule and seemed to be coming along nicely.

While in the city, Luis appeared in State Supreme Court in Manhattan before Justice Harold J. Rothwax. There he pleaded guilty to pulling his knife on a man on a subway platform on July 25, 1979, and stealing the man's oversized radio: armed robbery.

Justice Rothwax placed Luis on probation for five years. The judge said in an interview that he had done so in a plea-bargaining arrangement after being assured that Luis would spend the time in a locked facility.

But apparently there was a misunderstanding. Paul Elisha, a

continued

spokesman for the Division for Youth, said his agency was never directed to put Luis in a locked institution. He said youths sentenced to probation are invariably placed in unlocked facilities.

In any case, Luis returned to Great Valley.

Four months later, in February of this year, after he had been at Great Valley for 13 months, Luis was transferred to the state's Youth Development Center No. 2 in East Harlem; an unlocked six-story sandstone-and-brick building. There were 16 boys there. Luis stayed three days before taking flight.

He headed for his father's tenement apartment on the Lower East Side. On March 4, 1981, Felix Guzman returned his son to the center. He still has a tattered receipt for the boy.

"I left the same day," Luis said. This time he went to his mother's apartment.

Law enforcement officials say that a warrant was issued for Luis's arrest, that youth workers searched for him on the Lower East Side, to no avail.

Over the next seven months, Luis made a joke of the attempts to rehabilitate him. He roamed the streets with the "Little Wild Boys" gang, which eventually renamed itself "The Baddest Boys Around." He snatched gold chains on the Upper East Side, and he went out mugging with "my boys." He drifted in and out of his parents' apartments and the apartments of friends.

In April, Luis was arrested and charged with stealing a Father's Day plaque from a card shop on East 14th Street, the police said. The charge was conditionally dismissed and Luis went free. No one noticed the outstanding warrent against Luis for running away from the youth center.

In the summer, a policeman caught Luis trespassing on a contruction site, where he had gone to steal sheets of plywood. The policeman took Luis to his mother's apartment and let him go with a warning. That officer was also apparently unaware of the arrest warrant.

Shortly after the start of school in September, the police said, Luis stole a teacher's purse from a classroom at Junior High School 22, where his sister Evelyn is a student. An undercover policeman from the Seventh Precinct saw him sprinting down the street with the purse and took him into custody.

Sent to Rikers Island

He was taken to Rikers Island for the first time. But in four days he was free again after promising to appear in Criminal Court on Oct. 7. Once again, the arrest warrant had been overlooked.

Luis said he had intended to return to court on Oct. 7, but, he

continued

added, "then I got busted for this murder, something I didn't do."

"If I did it," he said, "I would admit it. I wouldn't be scared to admit it. Everytime I do a robbery I admit it."

At Rikers, after talking for more than two hours, sitting still, seldom even moving a hand, Luis began to twist and turn in his straight-backed chair. He was tired of the way his life had been going, too. He wanted to get out of New York, go to Puerto Rico.

"There's too much trouble around here," he said. "My boys be instigating. If I don't go with them they say, 'You're a sucker.' So I just go with them. But now when I get out of here, if I work this case, I ain't going to hang out with them. My mother's going to try to get me a ticket to Puerto Rico. I ain't never coming back."

—SOURCE: Joseph B. Treaster, "Crime at an Early Age: The Violent Streets of Luis Guzman." The New York Times, November 9, 1981, pp. B1 ff.

ADDITIONAL READINGS

Systems

Ackerman, N. J. (1984). *A theory of family systems.* New York: Gardner Press.

Anderson, R. E., & Carter, I. (1984). *Human behavior in the social environment: A social systems approach* (3rd ed.). New York: Aldine.

Barker, R. (1978). *Habitats, environments, and human behavior.* San Francisco: Jossey-Bass.

Bennis, W. G., Benne, K. D., Chin, R., & Corey, K. E. (Eds.). (1976). *The planning of change* (3rd ed.). New York: Holt, Rinehart and Winston.

Buckley, W. (1967). *Sociology and modern systems theory.* Englewood Cliffs, NJ: Prentice-Hall.

Durkin, J. (1981). *Living groups: Group psychotherapy and general systems theory.* New York: Brunner/Mazel.

Etzioni, A. (1964). *Modern organizations.* Englewood Cliffs, NJ: Prentice-Hall.

Laszlo, E. (1974). *The systems view of the world.* New York: Braziller.

Litterer, J. (Ed.). (1968). *Organizations: Systems, control and adaptation,* vol. 2 (2nd ed.). New York: Wiley.

Mackintosh, D. C. (1978). *Systems of health care.* Boulder, CO: Westview Press.

Miller, J. G. (1978). *Living systems.* New York: McGraw-Hill.

Parsons, T. (1964). *The social system.* New York: The Free Press.

Pincus, A., & Minahan, A. (1973). *Social work practice: Model and method.* Itasca, IL: F.E. Peacock Publishers.

Rothman, J., Elrich, J. L., & Teresa, J. G. (1976). *Promoting innovation and change in organizations and communities.* New York: Wiley.

Sauber, R. S. (1983). *The human services delivery system.* New York: Columbia University Press.

Human Diversity

Boggan, E. C., Foft, M. G., Lister, C., & Rupp, J. (1975). *The rights of gay people.* New York: Avon Books.

Bowe, F. (1978). *Handicapping America: Barriers to disabled people.* New York: Harper & Row.

Dana, R. H. (Ed.). (1981). *Human services for cultural minorities.* Baltimore: University Park Press.

Devore, W., & Schlesinger, E. C. (1981). *Ethnic sensitive social work practice.* St. Louis: C.V. Mosby.

Dougherty, M. C. (1978). *Becoming a woman in rural black culture.* New York: Holt, Rinehart and Winston.

Feagan, J. R., & Feagan, C. B. (1978). *Discrimination American style: Institutional racism and sexism.* Englewood Cliffs, NJ: Prentice Hall.

Gilligan, C. (1982). *In a different voice: Psychological theory and women in development.* Cambridge: Harvard University Press.

Gochros, H. L., & Gochros, J. S. (Eds.). (1977). *The sexually oppressed.* New York: Association Press.

Jenkins, S. (1981). *The ethnic dilemma in social services.* Riverside, NJ: The Free Press.

Katz, J. (1976). *Gay American history: Lesbians and gay men in the U.S.A.* New York: Avon Books.

Lique, K. H., (Ed.). (1982). *A mutual challange: Training and learning with the Indochinese in social work.* Boston University School of Social Work.

Long, E., Long J., Leon W., & Weston P. B. (1975). *American minorities: The justice issue.* Englewood Cliffs, NJ: Prentice-Hall.

Lowe, M., & Hubbard, R. (Eds.). (1983). *Woman's nature: Rationalizations of inequality.* New York: Pergamon Press.

Rothschild, J. (1983). *Machina Ex Dea: Feminist perspective on technology.* New York: Pergamon Press.

Schaef, A. W. (1981). *Women's reality: An emerging female system in the white male society.* Minneapolis: Winston Press.

Spender, D. (Ed.). (1981). *Men's studies modified: The impact of feminism on the academic disciplines.* New York: Pergamon Press.

Underwood, J. H. (1979). *Human variation and human micro evolution.* Englewood Cliffs, NJ: Prentice-Hall.

Walker, A. (1982). *The color purple.* New York: Harcourt, Brace, Jovanovich.

Goal-Directed Behavior

Berelson, B., & Steiner, G.A. (1967). *Human behavior: An inventory of scientific findings.* New York: Harcourt, Brace and World.

Bolles, R. C. (1975). *Theory of motivation* (2nd ed.). New York: Harper & Row.

Buhler, C., & Buhler, M. (Eds.). (1968). *The course of human life: A study of goals in the humanistic perspective.* New York: Springer Publishers.

Cofer, C. N. (1980) *Human motivation.* Detroit: Gale Publishing Co.

Maslow, A. (1976). *The farther reaches of human nature.* New York: Penguin Books.

Monat, A., & Lazarus, R. S. (Eds.). (1977). *Stress and coping: An anthology.* New York: Columbia University Press.

Russell, W. A. (Ed.). (1970). *Milestones in motivation: Contributions to the psychology of drive and purpose.* Englewood Cliffs, NJ: Prentice-Hall.

REFERENCES

Auletta, K. (1982). *The Underclass.* New York: Random House.

Brown, C. (1984, September 16). Manchild in Harlem. *The New York Times Magazine,* pp. 36ff.

Federico, R. (1984). *The social welfare institution* (4th ed.). Lexington, MA: D.C. Heath.

Fricke, A. (1981). *Reflections of a rock lobster.* Boston: Alyson Publishing Co.

Hanchett, E. (1979). *Community health assessment: A conceptual tool kit.* New York: Wiley.

Maslow, A. (1970). *Motivation and personality* (2nd ed.). New York: Harper & Row.

Meninger K. (1963). *The vital balance: The life process in mental health and illness.* New York: Viking Press.

Norton, D. (1978). *The dual perspective.* New York: Council on Social Work Education.

Pear, R. (1983, December 19). True hunger and malnutrition cases are growing problems, experts say. *The New York Times,* p. D15.

Stark, L. (1984, Spring). The homeless of Phoenix: 1984. *Southwest Reporter,* pp. 1ff. Arizona State University School of Social Work.

Stewart, R. (1984). From the president. *The NASW News, 29* (4), p. 2.

The New York Times. (1984, January 16). Women's wages lag further behind men's, pp. A1ff.

Towle, C. (1965). *Common human needs* (rev. ed.). New York: National Association of Social Workers.

4

HUMAN BEHAVIOR THROUGHOUT THE LIFE CYCLE

CHAPTER OVERVIEW

This chapter focuses on human behavior as an integrated whole throughout the life cycle. It begins with an analysis of what is meant by the term *life cycle,* and goes on to identify major life-cycle stages. From birth to death, behavior is shaped by societal expectations, subcultural values, and individual goals and aspirations. Each factor that shapes behavior does so by means of the resource systems discussed in the previous chapter. The result is progression through life according to a type of life-stage master plan that is partly biological, partly psychological, partly cultural, and partly social-structural. Understanding this master plan enables professional helping people to see how various life situations are likely to be troublesome at different points in the life cycle. This view also ties problems to the resources available to help address them. The chapter further emphasizes the special impact of human diversity throughout the life cycle.

DEFINING THE LIFE CYCLE

The concept of the **life cycle** is an easy one to understand: It refers to the period from conception to death, encompassing the totality of the physical, psychological, social-structural, and cultural experiences of living. Seen as a whole, the life cycle represents the aspirations people have about the potential of human life. Parents dream that their children will be happy and successful. Children dream that they will be rich and famous. Even communities and societies nurture collective dreams about what each generation can accomplish so that the whole group's quality of life will be improved. These dreams serve to motivate people, individually and collectively, in their efforts to move through the life cycle. Naturally, dreams do not always come true, but dreams die hard and they provide powerful incentives.

Throughout the life cycle, people utilize the biological, psychological, social-structural, and cultural resources that are available to them. These, in turn, serve to define the duration and quality of the life cycle. Death may occur at any time because of biological factors such as illness or genetically inherited limitations. Death may also result from personality disorders that drive troubled people to suicide, or from social-structural factors such as manufacturing processes that expose workers to fatal chemical toxins. Loss of life can even be caused by cultural beliefs. In some societies in the past, the elderly were expected to take their own lives when they became dependent on others. Today, members of some religious groups sacrifice their lives because of their beliefs about medicine, or their faith in people they consider prophets. On the other hand, of course, life can be prolonged and enriched by biological health and genetic strength, a stable and well-balanced personality, social-structural advantages such as wealth and social status, and cultural values that encourage mutual aid and support.

The life cycle is experienced in a unique way by each individual. Yet everyone shares **developmental tasks** that may be biological, psychological, or social-structural. These are processes or activities considered essential for the continued growth and maturation of the physical organism, as well as for its ability to adapt successfully to its social and physical environment. For example, all infants have to grow and develop biologically in order to survive. Humans also have to develop the psychological mechanisms through which they can manage the stress of daily life. The life cycle illustrates the relationship between common human needs and human diversity which was discussed in the last chapter. It shows how there are tasks that give direction to people's lives. The manner in which these tasks are performed, however, varies considerably between different groups. Many Americans dream of owning their own business, for example, as the preferred way of obtaining economic resources. Many Japanese aspire to life-long careers in a large corporation instead, achieving the same developmental task in a different way. In still other cases, there may be similarity in approaches used by all cultures. People everywhere long for a just and safe world where their children can grow up to be healthy and happy.

THE CONCEPT OF LIFE-CYCLE STAGES

Life-cycle stages are points in the life cycle that are associated with chronological age and developmental tasks. Each society has a conception of age, and differentiates people on that basis. In all societies, the young and the old are treated in different ways. For example, those who are older are expected to care for those who are younger, although at some point—usually called "old age"—the very old may be cared for by those who are younger. This age differentiation is based on recognition of the association of age with physical, mental, and social factors. In other words, the very young (and sometimes the very old) are believed to know less and to be able to do less than those who are in the middle age range. Societies believe that there is a physical and emotional process of maturation which is associated with age and which must occur before people can act as adults. Because most social behavior must be learned from others, time is required for this socialization process to occur. Current studies of stress in children are demonstrating that problems may result when demands are made on developing youngsters who are not yet ready to manage them, either physically or emotionally (Collins, 1983).

Although all societies have identified life-cycle stages, what they are varies greatly across societies (and even within the same society at different times) (Munroe & Munroe, 1975). In our own society, adulthood is reached at 18 or 21, according to various legal definitions. Yet the Jewish bar mitzvah, the ceremony that recognizes that a boy has become a man, occurs at age 13. Many nonindustrial societies expect young people to marry and start their own families during the mid-teens when they aquire adult sexual capacity. Even in this country, economic need may force adult responsibilities on children (as was the case with Veronica in the exhibit in Chapter 1). There is some similarity in the identification of life-cycle stages in Western industrialized societies (Bloom, 1980; Rogers, 1982), and bodies of theory support this view (Ganter & Yeakel, 1980; Langer, 1969). This is the approach to life-cycle stages that will be used in this book, but you should be vigilant for human diversity variables that may modify them in particular instances.

The principal significance of life-cycle stages is the way each emphasizes specific **life tasks,** activities that are considered necessary and/or desirable at particular points in the life cycle. Life tasks are defined by cultures and translated through social structures into expected behaviors. For example, in childhood there are cultural expectations about toilet training. These range from rigid definitions of when toilet training should occur in some groups, to very relaxed views about its importance in others. The expectations are translated into behaviors such as the use of various training devices and procedures. Children are praised for comforming to expectations and punished if they do not. Where the child's toilet behavior isn't considered important, it is likely to be ignored. When toilet behavior is perceived as a problem for a particular child, therapy may be sought.

If we can look at the life cycle as representing the aspirations that people have, perhaps life-cycle stages can be viewed as the master plan by which dreams come true—or are destroyed. As society (based on culture) defines life tasks, people's individual hopes get tested. When their goals differ from those of most others, they may experience considerable pressure to conform. Women who want careers instead of families experience this pressure at many life-cycle stages (Bernard, 1981). Or, the resources available at earlier life-cycle stages may affect the way future life tasks are experienced. The young child crippled by malnutrition caused by his/her family's poverty will have dreams of athletic glory or even good health shattered. Stage by stage, the life cycle gets shaped by biological, psychological, social-structural, and cultural factors. In the end, life may have been perceived as a dream or a nightmare.

Some life tasks change as people move through life-cycle stages. Children, for instance, are not expected to be economically self-supporting, whereas adults are not expected to relate to others with the degree of selfishness we accept from children. As we have seen, these differences reflect, in part, changing age-related biological and psychological needs and capacities. However, other life tasks remain with us throughout the life cycles, for example, we have to meet our basic physical needs. As children we do so by relying heavily on others, whereas adults attempt to be independent, and the elderly often have to find some balance between dependence and independence. Similarly, the task of relating to others is accomplished differently at each stage in the life cycle, but it remains a life-long task. As children we selfishly love those on whom we depend. As adults, our ability to relate to loved ones is based more on reciprocity and intimacy. We can also see similar changes throughout the life cycle in the life-long tasks of developing a sense of psychological well-being and environmental mastery.

The similarities and changes we have been discussing must, of

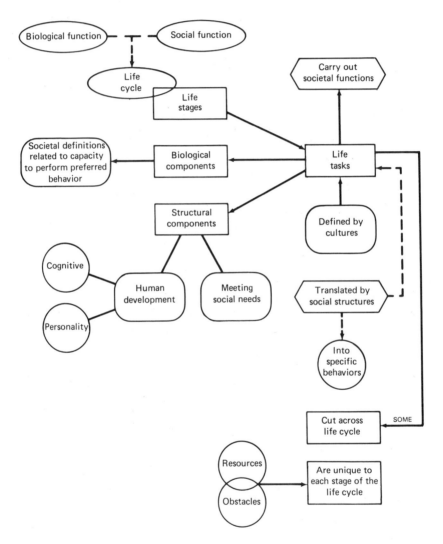

FIGURE 4.1—Life Cycle

course, be understood within the context of human diversity. Consider speech, for illustrative purposes. We generally learn to speak in early childhood, and as we get older we gradually expand our range of speech as well as those with whom we speak. Within this general framework there are many variations. We may learn one language or several. Some people have to relearn how to speak because of damage to their vocal apparatus caused by illness or injury. Some deaf people learn to speak long after childhood when their deafness is better understood and appropriate surgical and/or educational resources are available. Others continue to use their ability to "speak" through sign language they learned as children. And still other people are blocked from speaking by the barrier of autism. It cannot be emphasized enough that human behavior in specific situations must be carefully analyzed within the context of human diversity. Any attempt to conceptualize human behavior during the life cycle as something that occurs in a similar way to everyone inevitably overlooks the richness of human diversity. Life-cycle stages are simply devices to help us understand how human life becomes a totality of biological, psychological, cultural, and social-structural factors. Stages are not rigid and universal for all groups. Developed for this book by Dee Thornberry, Figure 4.1 presents an overview of the life cycle and shows the many elements involved in it. It should help you to pull together the content from previous chapters and to begin to apply it to your developing understanding of the life cycle.

BIOLOGICAL POTENTIAL AND THE LIFE CYCLE

We have already reviewed much about the biological basis for behavior. You know that human beings are enormously adaptable because of their genetic inheritance. This establishes limits or, seen more positively, potential for behavior. Humans can learn to do many things and to flourish in many types of environments. The human organism changes throughout the life cycle, experiencing rapid growth until late childhood followed by a period of much slower growth until late adolescence (Troll, 1975). Organic deterioration begins with life itself, but accelerates from middle adulthood until it culminates in death (Kalish, 1975). Of course, the environmental conditions that either promote health or impede it interact in important ways with biological growth and deterioration.

In Chapter 3 systems of resources and obstacles were discussed. Biological potential during the life cycle is best understood in terms of the user system, especially in instances when users of services are individuals. People bring their own unique characteristics to the situations they confront. These characteristics, as you know, are biological, psychological, cultural, and social-structural, but for now we will focus on the biological. The biological potential that people have gives particular meaning to their encounter with each life-cycle stage. We have seen that there are tasks, or expectations associated with each stage. Some are biological, such as the expectation that children will get taller, will develop the ability to see and hear clearly, and will be able to walk and use their limbs to perform various activities. Those who meet these expectations are considered "normal" and receive social approval. In this instance, their biological capacity is a **resource** because it enables them to accomplish life tasks and goals.

When expectations cannot be met because of biological limits, these limits may be seen as **obstacles.** This can occur with children who are blind, deaf, or without limbs that they can control. In these cases the biological expectations of childhood become problematic, and help may be needed. Note that we are talking only about *societal expectations* developed for everyone, and the way that *individuals* with particular biological abilities experience them. This is a far different perspective than one that views the individual as being at fault or inadequate. The ability to meet expectations is simply a reflection of access to resources, in this case biological resources, but we will see that the basic process is the same when looking at other resource systems. The fact that people have different resources says little about them as worthy people. It does, however, help us as professional helpers to understand what obstacles they are likely to encounter. Indeed, it would be more realistic and more humane to change the expectation that everyone be alike rather than to force people with varying resources to try to compete with each other.

So far we have been talking about socially defined biological expectations and the way they interact with biological resources and obstacles. But there are also psychological, cultural, and social-structural expectations at each life cycle stage. Adolescents, for example, are expected to achieve enough psychological maturity to function with increasing degrees of independence from their parents (Erikson, 1968). Social-structural expectations at this stage include completing high school and moving into advanced education or employment. Biological resources of individuals are relevant in all these instances. An adolescent with a physical limitation that requires extra care from others may find it more difficult to become independent. Completing school and making future study or work plans is also made more difficult for adolescents whose intellectual capacity, which is in part genetic, is so limited as to make the demands of formal schooling unusually taxing.

Many of the examples used so far have illustrated how the biological characteristics of people limit their ability to meet expectations associated with life-cycle stages. Naturally, the reverse of a limitation would be a resource, or a help. Limited intellect often makes school difficult and frustrating, while high intelligence often makes it easier and more rewarding. Thus, both resources and obstacles affect people's ability to meet expectations, although they do so in opposite ways. However, another aspect of this relationship is also relevant. Biological characteristics that are resources with respect to some expectations will be obstacles for others. Let's look again at the expectations of adolescence noted above. The adolescent who is gifted intellectually may find school exhilarating and rewarding. However, s/he may also be defined as a "bookworm," or resented by less-gifted peers. As a result, s/he might find it difficult establishing friendships with peers. This can, in turn, weaken the adolescent's self-concept as well as reduce the emotional support from peers that is often helpful when beginning to establish independence from parents. In this instance, then, it is evident how a resource is also an obstacle. At this point it is suggested that you take a moment to think through an example that illustrates that the reverse is also true, in other words, that an obstacle may be a resource.

Once again, the importance of human diversity should be noted. People not only bring different resources and obstacles to life-cycle stage expectations; their perception of the expectations may differ (Green, 1982). This reflects cultural and subcultural variations in defining what is expected. For example, American culture tends to idealize the image of men with broad shoulders, slim women with large breasts, and anyone with blond hair ("blonds have more fun"). Other cultures prefer men who are tall, women who we would consider fat, and black hair. Such biological features are in themselves of no special significance, but they become resources or obstacles when they are defined by cultures as desirable or unappealing. Human behavior is rich and complex. We must always remember that there are many variations even as we try to understand the general ways in which behavior becomes organized through the operation of expectations, resources, and obstacles associated with each life-cycle stage.

PSYCHOLOGICAL DEVELOPMENT AND THE LIFE CYCLE

To review briefly, psychological functioning is concerned with perception, cognition, and the personality structure's integration of biological imperatives and socially imposed demands. The psychological dimensions of human behavior, then, make it possible for people to understand themselves and their environments. This is of great importance given the need for humans as social beings to adapt to the environment in which they happen to live.

As with biological growth, psychological development is guided by a set of expectations tied to life-cycle stages. The psychological expectations associated with life-cycle stages have been formulated by many theorists, including Freud, Erikson, and Piaget among the most prominent (Baldwin, 1968; Langer, 1969; Norbeck, Price-Williams, & McCord, 1968; Wadsworth, 1979). Although these theories are not identical, they agree that expectations for psychological development are tied to the life-cycle stages. They begin in infancy with the development of self-awareness and perception of the immediate environment, move into concern with cognition and relationships with others during childhood, and focus on further cognitive growth, life direction, and intimate relationships in adolescence. The psychological expectations for adulthood and old age have been thoroughly detailed (Brody, 1983; Kalish, 1975; Levinson, 1979; Troll, 1975). Nevertheless, expectations of stability and productivity in adulthood, and managing loss in late adulthood and old age have been identified as being of particular importance.

Resources and obstacles are critical as people attempt to meet these expectations. Consider the very difficult loss management involved in confronting one's own death. Psychological resources could include awareness of the need to prepare for death, satisfaction with what has been accomplished during life, and a strong self-concept that can accept the ultimate loss of self through death. Because dying is a social as well as biological and psychological phenomenon, a number of cultural and social-structural resources help to manage loss. Spiritual or religious beliefs that allow people to perceive death as a non-threatening state are comforting (cultural beliefs). Knowing that loved ones are cared for is also reassuring (social-structural arrangements). Even the conditions of one's own death are important. Being in physical pain from a terminal illness, something that we would generally see as a biological obstacle, may be a resource if it helps people accept death as the end of their suffering. Receiving loving and humane care from family, friends, and medical personnel, which again relates to social-structural factors, can also make the acceptance of death easier.

Psychological resources and obstacles are pertinent when confronting other types of life-cycle stage expectations. We already saw how the expectation for adults to be physically independent can be problematic for handicapped people, but how personality strength is a resource in finding solutions. We also saw how the social-structural expectation for adolescents to develop a peer network can be affected by intelligence as a psychological (and biological) resource. Again and again we come back to the holistic nature of human life. Understanding any kind of behavior demands that its context also be understood.

CULTURE, SOCIAL STRUCTURES, AND THE LIFE CYCLE

So far we have looked at sources of life-cycle stage expectations that pertain primarily to one system, the user system, and specifically to individuals as users. Now we can look at a more complex case, where several systems become involved in defining and meeting expectations. Social structures, as we saw in Chapter 2, organize behavior through such entities as families, communities, bureaucracies, friendship groups, and so on. These flow from a society's culture, which establishes basic principles of *what* people ought to do and *how* they should do it. For example, how we should interact with those we love is defined through family and family-like structures that influence our behavior. This is a primary reason why divorce can be so painful—it leaves us doubting our ability to love others, and disconnected from social relationships that have been very significant for us (Brody, 1983).

Life-cycle expectations range from those stated rather broadly (the well should help the sick) to those which apply to very specific situations (a nurse should give the proper medicine to a patient in his/her care). For example, children are expected to go to school. There several things are supposed to occur: children learn to relate to adults other than parents; children learn to form friendships with other children; and children learn more about themselves, their world, and their society. These are social expectations entrusted to a specific social structure—the school. The biological and psychological characteristics of both children and teachers affect whether these expectations are met. Also, the way the school itself is organized interacts with these characteristics. Segregated schools may help reinforce the self-perception of minority children as being inferior. Low-quality education (which is sometimes provided in such schools) supports this perception, and makes it more difficult for minority children to be successful in later schooling and in the work place.

In Chapter 3 other social-structural systems of paticular concern to professional helpers were discussed. These include helping professions, social agencies, the social welfare institution, society as a system, communities, and families/family-like units. Each system carries within it socially defined life-cycle stage expectations, as well as resources and obstacles relevant to them. We can see schools as part of the community system, and we have shown how they relate to societal and cultural expectations. Consider the family as another example. Our culture expects young adults to establish families or family-like units. This requires the ability to form intimate relationships with others, to function as financially independent adults, to fulfill the parental role if appropriate, and so on. As with the school, we can see how the translation of cultural values into societal expectations is tied to specific life-cycle stages and implemented through the social structure. As noted earlier, these in turn relate to the biological and psychological characteristics of individuals. (To understand this point, look at a social agency as a social structure. Work step-by-step to explain how it relates to social/cultural expectations for a life-cycle stage of your choice.)

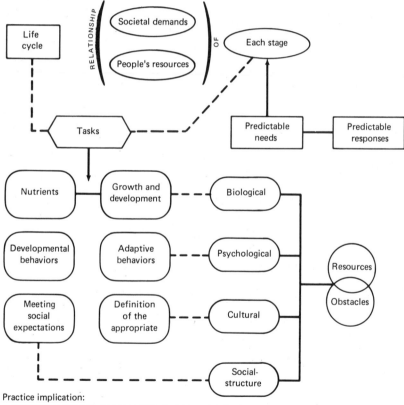

Practice implication:
  Intervention between people and the environment-behaviors are
  perceived as helpful or problematic.

FIGURE 4.2—Life Cycle Stages

In addition to defining expectations, social structures also serve as resources and obstacles for their attainment. Young adults are expected to form families, but their efforts to do so are influenced by whether they are employed in a job that provides a steady and sufficient income, the emotional support they get from family and friends, their opportunities to meet potential mates, and so forth. Adults with families are expected to care for their young, but they may lack the financial resources, good health, physical ability, or emotional strength to do so. In such instances, social agencies, families, and friendship groups may be important social-structural resources to help overcome biological, psychological, and social-structural obstacles. Obviously, social-structural expectations, resources, and obstacles interact with the biological and psychological ones examined earlier in this chapter.

To conclude this section, Figure 4.2 presents another illustration prepared for this book by Dee Thornberry. It presents the many pieces of the life cycle and life-cycle stages that have to be understood in order to comprehend behavior in a holistic way. It summarizes and integrates material from this and earlier chapters, and is a helpful foundation for what will follow.

IDENTIFYING LIFE-CYCLE STAGES

We have talked a great deal about life-cycle stages. Now we are ready to list the ones that will be used in the remainder of this book. They are the following: conception and birth, infancy and early childhood (from birth to about 4), middle and late childhood (from about 4 to 12), adolescence (from about 13 to 18), young adulthood (from about 18 to 25), middle adulthood (from about 25 to 45), late adulthood (from about 45 to 61), retirement, and death. Stages are defined in this way for purely illustrative and analytical purposes. They reflect social definitions and expectations used in this society, not any universals in human life (because there are wide cultural variations in definitions of life-cycle stages). Probably the only two universals are conception and death. What occurs between them can vary from miscarriage (death before birth), to death at birth, to death at any point up through old age.

This chapter ends with a reminder that the importance of life-cycle stages is their utility for understanding in a holistic way how and why people sometimes need help. Any practice situation involves people who are trying to meet expectations for a given stage in the life-cycle. Their efforts to do so are heavily influenced by the resources and obstacles that are part of their situation. Life situations often involve people who are at different points in the life cycle. Behavior in the family provides a good example: Parents are concerned with issues such as demonstrating their ability to succeed in the work place, redefining relationships with their aging parents (who may be gradually becoming more physically dependent on others), and transmitting deeply held values to their children. Teenage children in the family may be struggling to become more independent, and so may resist the teachings of their parents or the emerging needs for assistance by their grandparents. Younger family members, who still need a sense of security and psychological nuturing, may react fearfully to what seems to them to be conflict between their elder siblings and their parents and grandparents. The juxtaposition of people at several life-cycle stages generates very complex networks of behavior. Different people seek to meet different needs by using different resources, yet all the while they are attempting to maintain social patterns that are useful for everyone.

It is no small task for the helping professional to understand all of this. If helping people could focus on one life-cycle stage at a time, the helper's task would be easier. But the holistic nature of human life and human systems creates multifaceted behaviors which occur simultaneously and have an impact on each other. As a result, multiple life-cycle stages are frequently involved in the same practice situation, and each must be understood both singly and in interaction. For example, in the family described above, any day-to-day situation would involve each family member's efforts to meet his/her life-cycle needs as well as the impact of those behaviors on the need-meeting activities of the other family members. Chapter 5 will present a useful framework for analyzing life-cycle stages and thus disentangling all these pieces. Before moving on, however, Exhibit 4.1, which ends this chapter, describes how the Hunt family tries to obtain and use resources to meet the needs of its members who are at several different life-cycle stages. As you will see, the many obstacles faced by this family make the task a difficult one.

SUMMARY

The chapter has explored the concepts of the life cycle and life-cycle stages in some depth. These refer respectively to the total life span, and to periods throughout the life span to which society allocates specific tasks and functions. At each each of these periods, socially defined expectations exist which include biological, psychological, social-structural, and cultural phenomena. They reflect, in a general way, the biological capacity of the human being and the cultural values of society that define certain things as more necessary than others. In attempting to meet the expectations that are organized around the stages of the life cycle, people make use of resources while also trying to overcome obstacles. These, like the expectations, may be biological, psychological, social-structural, and cultural. The life situations that bring users to helping professionals can best be understood in terms of the interaction of expectations, resources, and obstacles at each life-cycle stage. In this way, human behavior is seen in its rich but complex wholeness, a view that is critical for the generalist helping professional.

STUDY QUESTIONS

1. Have you thought about your own life cycle and developed tentative plans for what you would like to accomplish? Try to analyze what factors have influenced your thinking about what you would like your life to be like. What assumptions have you made about the resources you will have available to help you accomplish your goals for yourself?

2. Analyze your own family in terms of life-cycle stages. Take each person in your family and identify his/her life-cycle stage. For each, identify as many expectations as you can, making sure to include biological, psychological, social-structural, and cultural expectations. And don't forget to include yourself!

3. Think about the resources that you have. Write down four headings: biological, psychological, social-structural, and cultural. Under each, list as many resources as you can that you think you have. Now compare your list with that of a classmate. How similar are your lists? Why?

4. Repeat exercise number 3 above, but substitute obstacles for resources. Do you find it easier or harder to think about obstacles? Why?

5. Interview someone who is 60 or older. Develop a set of questions that will enable you to understand how that person has viewed his/her own life cycle. You might consider questions that ask about the happiest time of your life, the most significant, the most difficult, life satisfactions, and so on. Then ask your respondent to discuss his/her plans for the future. Try to see how the future is viewed, and the resources that are perceived as likely to be available.

KEY TERMS

Developmental tasks Processes or activities considered essential for the continued growth and maturation of the physical organism, as well as for its ability to adapt successfully to its social and physical environment. Developmental tasks may be biological, psychological, or social-structural.

Life cycle The period from conception to death, encompassing the totality of the physical, psychological, social-structural, and cultural experiences of living.

Life-cycle stages Selected points in the life cycle that are associated with chronological age and developmental tasks.

Life tasks Activities that are considered necessary and/or desirable at various points in the life cycle.

Obstacle Anything that interferes with people's efforts to accomplish their life tasks and goals.

Resource Anything that enables people to accomplish their life tasks and goals.

This exhibit looks at the Hunt family's efforts to survive on public assistance. Three life-cycle stages are represented: middle adulthood (Mrs. Hunt), early adulthood (her two sons), and late childhood (her daughter). Life on public assistance creates serious obstacles to meeting life tasks and life-cycle expectations. However, this case is an interesting example of obstacles and resources. The obstacles are what might be expected: nutritional limits (biological), feelings of inferiority because of being poor (psychological), and poverty (social-structural). However, the resources are substantial, too: tremendous energy to walk long distances to shop as economically and wisely as possible (biological), what is described as "spiritual armor" (psychological), and participation in supportive networks of friends and other welfare mothers (social-structural). The Hunt family, then, is a good example of how life-cycle tasks, expectations, resources, and obstacles get played out in the real world.

4.1 THE HUNT FAMILY

After buying necessities and paying bills, Sharon Hunt had $11 left from her welfare check. But there was an unexpected expense for her baby, Tanya.

Miss Hunt said the 13-month-old child's synthetic—blend pajamas, purchased as "great bargains," were causing a rash. "I'm going to have to break down and buy her some cotton nightgowns even though we'll have less money to last until the next check comes in about two weeks," she said.

Miss Hunt said she went back on welfare about five months ago for the first time in 10 years after Federal budget cuts eliminated her job at New York Community Advocacy Research and Development, a food and nutrition program.

A Painful Choice

As is generally the case for welfare recipients and other poor people, narrow choices and hidden costs of poverty have been insistent bullies in the lives of Miss Hunt and her children. Even after developing a spiritual armor that helped them through tough times, she said, it is still painful to have to decide between the lesser of two evils.

Martin Burdick, acting deputy administrator of the city's income maintenance programs, says that because of the effect

continued

that inflation has had on public-assistance grants, making do is more difficult for the poor these days. And difficult decisions are more plentiful.

"I have to give my kids more than hard times for a diet," Miss Hunt said.

Several social-service and welfare groups were asked to recommend a welfare recipient who would be willing to discuss the family's budget and its strategy for living on public assistance. Miss Hunt, a short woman with electric energy, is a welfare-rights activist who agreed to discuss her finances in detail.

She allowed a reporter to accompany her to a welfare center, where she was required to establish her eligibility for continued public assistance. She must go through this procedure three times a year. There was no way to verify independently that she had no other sources of income. It also could not be determined whether she might have been able to find a job that would pay enough to get off welfare.

Over several recent days in her Manhattan apartment and on shopping trips, Miss Hunt had to decide between a cold child and a rash, between buying what was on sale and what her family actually needed, between not meeting her family's needs and going deeper into debt.

The 40-year-old mother

scoured advertisements for the coupons she clips, picked through bins of damaged goods at bargain stores for clothing for her children and walked more than a mile for a bargain on a detergent.

Miss Hunt said she avoids public transportation unless it is absolutely necessary. She also is unable to budget for entertainment nor does she have a reserve for emergencies.

"Sharon really does the best she can for her family, probably better than I could do," said Mary Bighorse, program director of the American Indian Community House, a multiservice center in New York City. She has known Miss Hunt for about five years. "Considering her circumstances, it's a miracle that she makes it," she said.

Two Checks a Month

Miss Hunt receives a monthly welfare grant of $340 in two separate $170 checks, one at the beginning of the month and one in the middle, for herself, Tanya and a 10-year-old daughter, Kayla.

After $110 is deducted to pay the rent for her public-housing apartment on the Lower East Side, Miss Hunt's total welfare grant leaves about $2.55 in cash a day for each member of the family. Her food-stamp allotment is $115 a month, or about $1.28 a day for each

continued

family member, amounting to about 43 cents for each of three meals.

After receiving her first $170 check and the food stamps one week, she went about juggling them and her stamina in an effort to survive. She gathered the check, stamps and supermarket coupons, bundled up Tanya in the stroller she had borrowed money to buy, and prepared to walk from her home on Franklin D. Roosevelt Drive at East Houston Street to a supermarket on Avenue A and Fourth Street that was advertising specials.

Twice as Expensive

As is generally the case in most poor neighborhoods, she said, nearby corner markets offered goods that were twice as expensive and of lesser quality than those she could find outside her immediate area.

Miss Hunt had $1 in cash the day the welfare check arrived. The family had only a few cans of tuna, some boxes of instant macaroni and cheese, some beef pot pies, spinach and eggs. There were also the ever-present canisters of rice and beans, which Miss Hunt calls her "safety net" against hunger.

On this cold day, Kayla had worn to school the pair of boots she shares with her mother. So Miss Hunt put on a pair of thin, cloth-topped shoes she had bought for $1 at a bargain shop.

Along the route to the supermarket, which took her and her baby past knots of drug addicts, abandoned and graffiti-scarred buildings and vacant lots, Miss Hunt stopped at a storefront check-cashing business and paid $1.38 to cash her welfare check and an additional 95 cents for a $110 money order for her rent. She said grocery stores would not cash her welfare check.

She was then left with $57.67 in cash and the food stamps.

In the supermarket, she rolled her shopping cart past fresh vegetables and meats and loaded it with canned tuna and vegetables, cereal, baby food, bread and other items on sale.

Miss Hunt said she checks advertised specials and clips coupons before going to the supermarket. Once there, she said, she usually selects items on sale that are rich in protein, nonperishable and inexpensive.

Experience and Necessity

She purchases fresh vegetables and fruits only "when there is a really good buy," she said. While her former job in the nutrition program reinforced her knowledge of what constitutes a good diet, she said, it was "practical experience and absolute necessity" that shaped her current shopping habits.

continued

She paused at the poultry section and thought for a while before putting two chickens into her basket.

"Darwin is coming home from college this weekend, so maybe I can fix chicken for him on Sunday," she said. Darwin, who at 20 is her oldest child, is a student at the State University College at Old Westbury, L.I. He works and receives Federal and state grants to pay for his education and living expenses.

Another son, Maurice, is a dishwasher and security guard in Atlantic City.

After the cashier rang up the bill, Miss Hunt handed over $53.62 in food stamps and $2.33 in cash for items that the stamps did not cover. She was left with $61.38 in food stamps and $55.34 in cash.

Surplus Cheese and a Hat

On the way home, she stopped at a community center to sign up for the state program for the distribution of cheese from the Federal Government's surplus and at a Salvation Army store, where she bought a hat for 49 cents and a cooking pot for $1.29. This left her with $53.56 in cash.

Miss Hunt looked briefly at a small coat and hat that cost $4.05.

"That would fit the baby next year, but I don't have money to spend on something for next year," she said.

The next day she walked an even greater distance, to 14th Street near the Avenue of the Americas, to buy a detergent on sale at $1.56. And after paying $20 on a $350 debt and about $21 for her telephone bill, she had $11 in cash.

"I've lived without a telephone in the past and there have been times when I didn't have a dime to call somebody when my babies and I needed help," Miss Hunt said, explaining why she spends money for a telephone.

She also bought milk, juice, applesauce and other foods at a cost of $14.38 in food stamps, leaving her with $47 in stamps for the next two weeks.

In Debt to a Friend

Not unlike other welfare recipients, who often have to find additional means of support through family and friends, she is in debt to a friend.

The friend, who helped her when she had no income for seven weeks while applying for welfare, continues to help when she is in financial trouble.

But Miss Hunt says she still has difficulty adjusting to the anxiety that hits her when one of her sons visits and in one day drinks the juice that was meant to last for five, or when the baby

continued

screams in the night and there is no money for emergencies.

"It shouldn't hurt to be born in America," Miss Hunt observed. "It does, though. My salvation has been my children and my activities as a welfare-rights activist."

'Able to Fight' for Rights

"Welfare mothers have to organize," she said. "I've been able to fight for my rights through the help of the Redistribute America Movement." The group is a statewide poor people's organization.

"My life," Miss Hunt added, "has been hard, but my stuff is light compared to some people's stuff."

Kayla, whose youthful energy seems tempered by a sense of responsibility, says she enjoys having her mother at home rather than out working when she returns from school. But the family's financial situation has sometimes made Kayla the target of other children's insensitive comments.

"Sometimes the kids at school tease me," she said softly. "They ask me why I wear the same pants all the time or why I never have money for candy when we go to the store.

"I tell them if you don't like me the way I am, then we just can't be friends. A lot of the kids ask, 'Why are you on welfare?' And they say that we're living off the government. But I tell them we're just trying to survive, that's all."

How One Family Spent Its Welfare Allotment

Sharon Hunt receives a monthly welfare grant of $340 in two separate $170 checks, one at the beginning and one in the middle of each month. She also gets a monthly food stamp allotment of $116. Expenditures below show what she paid in the first half month.

Rent	$110.00
Check-cashing fee	1.38
Money order to pay rent	0.95
Groceries not covered by food stamps	2.33
Hat	0.49
Cooking Pot	1.29
Detergent	1.56
Personal debt	20.00
Telephone bill	21.00
Cash after expenses	11.00
CHECK TOTAL	**$170.00**

—SOURCE: Sheila Rule, "Family tries with welfare to 'make do'. The New York Times, *March 23, 1982, pp. B1ff.*

REFERENCES

Baldwin, A. (1968). *Theories of child development.* New York: Wiley.

Bernard, J. (1981). *The female world.* New York: The Free Press.

Bloom, M. (1980). *Life span development.* New York: Macmillan.

Brody, J. (1981, July 12). Personal health. *The New York Times,* p. C8.

Brody, J. (1983, December 13). Divorce's stress exacts long-term health toll. *The New York Times,* p. C1.

Collins, G. (1983, October 3). Children and stress: a search for causes. *The New York Times,* p. B12.

Erikson, E. (1968). *Identity: Youth and crisis.* New York: W. W. Norton.

Ganter, G., & Yeakel, M. (1980). *Human behavior and the social environment.* New York: Columbia University Press.

Green, J. (1982). *Cultural awareness in the human services.* Englewood Cliffs, NJ: Prentice-Hall.

Kalish, R. (1975). *Late adulthood: Perspectives on human development.* Monterey, CA: Brooks-Cole Publishers.

Langer, J. (1969). *Theories of development.* New York: Holt, Rinehart and Winston.

Levinson, D. (1979). *Seasons of a man's life.* New York: Ballantine Books.

Munroe, R., & Munroe, R. (1975). *Cross-cultural human development.* Monterey, CA: Brooks-Cole Publishers.

Norbeck, E., Price-Williams, D., & McCord, W. (1968). *The study of personality.* New York: Holt, Rinehart and Winston.

Rogers, D. (1982). *Life-span human development.* Monterey, CA: Brooks-Cole Publishers.

Troll, L. (1975). *Early and middle adulthood.* Monterey, CA: Brooks-Cole Publishers.

Wadsworth, B. (1979). *Piaget's theory of cognitive development* (2nd ed.). New York: Longman Inc.

5

UNDERSTANDING THE LIFE CYCLE: A MODEL FOR PRACTICE

- SUMMARY
- STUDY QUESTIONS
- KEY TERMS
- EXHIBIT 5.1: MAN-O-PAUSE: THE CLIMAC-TERIC IN MEN
- EXHIBIT 5.2: POVERTY
- ADDITIONAL READINGS
- REFERENCES

CHAPTER OVERVIEW

The life cycle, as pointed out in the last chapter, serves as a useful concept for understanding the person-environment trans-actions that characterize the central purpose of the helping professions. The expectations and demands imposed by society, and the accessibility of resources to meet the needs accompanying each stage of the life cycle create reasonably predictable patterns of behavior. Professional intervention may be necessary to remove obstacles to functioning and to diminish social risks, or to develop resources and create opportunities that will facilitate an individual's progression through the stages of the life cycle. However, the human diversity variables stressed throughout this book should be kept in mind. Practitioners need to be cautious in interpreting life-cycle theories too rigidly, remembering that individuals progress through these stages at varying paces, and that cultural variations often occur.

This chapter will present a model for conceptualizing life-cycle stages, then discuss each specific stage in more detail. Attention will be given to the resources and obstacles that facilitate or impede successful completion of life-cycle tasks. Exhibits 5.1 and 5.2 at the end of the chapter serve as springboards for further discussion of life-cycle events.

RECIPROCITY AND HISTORICAL COHORT

Newman and Newman (1984) discuss the importance of the concepts **reciprocity** and **historical cohort** to an understanding of the life cycle. Reciprocity, in this context, referes to mutuality and interdependence in social roles. Any setting in which individuals find themselves is populated by participants at different life-cycle stages, often involving such reciprocal roles as parent-child or teacher-student. Families, too, are composed of individuals who are at different developmental stages, sometimes resulting in problematic interaction (Newman & Newman, 1984). A teenage parent, for instance, may find responding to the developmental needs of an infant or toddler especially difficult if he/she is enmeshed in the psychosocial conflicts of adolescence. If resources and opportunities are not made available to the teenage parent, the reciprocal roles of parent and child may become plagued with conflict and tension.

Consider the life-cycle needs involved in an intergenerational household composed of adults in midlife caring for their aging parents and their adolescent children simultaneously. The differing role and affective expectations inherent in such a family setting may create tensions and conflicts in the caregivers. They are often assuming two different sets of responsibilities, one toward their aging parents and the other toward their children. This is not to say that intergenerational living arrangements are inevitably conflictual. Quite the contrary. Lowy (1983) points out that for many families such interdependence between and among generations is mutually beneficial to each generation, and is sometimes economically necessary. The potential for intimacy and sharing in intergenerational living arrangements is without question. Professional helping efforts, however, are often necessary to overcome obstacles.

A historical cohort is a "group that is born at about the same time and is exposed to a similar social, economic, political and cultural context" (Rosow, 1978). Newman and Newman (1984, p. 41) point out that an understanding of historical cohort groupings is important in order to answer questions about "whether people who are in a certain period of life are systematically different from those who are younger or older."

The concept of cohort is helpful in that it intersects individual life cycles with a historical time-line (Kimmel, 1980, p. 22). As cohort groups move through the life cycle, their shared experiences may color their interpretation of life-cycle events. The men and women who served in the Armed Forces during the Vietnam war, for instance, probably experience the role of veteran differently than veterans of previous wars. A specific behavioral pattern, therefore, may be heavily influenced by cohort variables. It may appear in one group as it progresses through a specific stage in the life cycle but may not be in evidence in previous or subsequent generations.

A FRAMEWORK FOR ANALYZING THE LIFE CYCLE

The generalist practitioner, in order to assess situations holistically, needs a systematic way of organizing information.

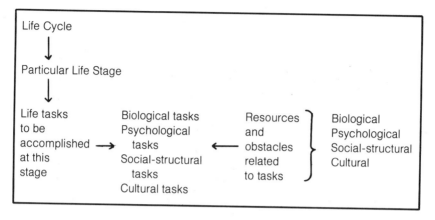

FIGURE 5.1—A Framework for Analyzing the Life Cycle

Figure 5.1 presents a way of visually conceptualizing the life cycle using concepts introduced earlier in this book.

The framework of Figure 5.1 focuses on life tasks as defined biologically (obtaining life-sustaining nutrients, as well as realizing biological capacities for growth and development), psychologically (accomplishing developmental and adaptive behaviors), social-structurally (meeting social expectations), and culturally (learning the accepted definitions of the appropriate). For each type of task at each stage of the life cycle, the practitioner needs to identify the significant resources and obstacles encountered. These resources or obstacles are biological, psychological, social-structural and cultural in nature, and reflect the systems, human diversity, and goal-directed behaviors that form the context of practice. When properly applied, this framework provides the kind of holistic view of human behavior that is consistent with the goals of professional practice—especially the goal of improving the transactions between people and environments.

Furthermore, such a model gives the professional a perspective that places human behavior in its wider context. Human life involves a constant interplay of biological, psychological, sociostructural and cultural forces working toward meeting individual, group, organizational, and societal goals. This interplay is dramatically played out at various life-cycle stages as resources are brought to bear, or as obstacles are encountered as people struggle to achieve tasks. Social welfare services are a specific kind of resource that facilitate successful completion of life-cycle tasks, sometimes by removing obstacles, and sometimes by creating new opportunities. Examples will be given throughout this chapter that illustrate how social welfare services facilitate accomplishing life-cycle tasks. Table 5.1 presents a way of analyzing each specific stage of the life cycle, focusing on the tasks to be accomplished and the resources or obstacles that facilitate or impede their accomplishment.

Before beginning a more detailed analysis of each specific stage in the life cycle, we will review some of the concepts presented in earlier chapters that will help us understand life-stage tasks, resources, and obstacles. Remember the purpose of this analysis is to help you, as a practitioner, to assess the quality of the person-environment transaction that is the focal point of professional intervention.

Biological tasks include such things as obtaining sufficient nutrients and assuring protection from physical abuse. These tasks are played out differently at different life stages. An example of a biological obstacle is substance abuse, which affects the desire to eat, as well as the body's ability to process nutrients. It also encompasses certain types of congenital birth defects that affect one's ability to protect oneself in the environment. Biological variables are those physiological characteristics that affect the ability of the organism to meet its needs through interaction with the environment. Assessing the quality of person-environment transaction from a biological standpoint necessitates an analysis of these variables.

Psychological tasks to be accomplished include obtaining sufficient nurturance, developing a healthy self-esteem, maintaining interpersonal relationships, and coping with stress. Psychological resources that accelerate the accomplishment of these tasks include adequate levels of cognitive and perceptual functioning. Certain types of personality disorders, learning disabilities, and intellectual impairments are examples of obstacles that would impede goal achievement. Psychological variables, then, are those characteristics that affect the ability of the organism to perceive, process, and interact with the environment.

TABLE 5.1—A FRAMEWORK FOR ANALYZING EACH STAGE IN THE LIFE CYCLE

Source of behavior	Examples of given stages and related tasks	Factors affecting task performance	
		Obstacles	Resources
Biological	Conception and birth: healthy pregnancy and delivery	Poor prenatal care	Good health, nutrition
	Infancy and early childhood: mastery over body; language learning	Inherited disabilities	Parenting; physical well-being
Psychological	Conception and birth: readiness to be a parent	Immaturity	Knowledge about parenthood
	Infancy: relating to family and others	Stress	Parenting techniques
Social-structural	Conception and birth: availability of prenatal health care	Inadequate safeguards in environment	Tax benefits; health care
	Infancy: learning to relate to family members	Inadequate care	Social stimulation, medical care
Cultural	Conception and birth: preparing to carry out the parental role in socially-approved ways	Being unwed and/or unsupported	Being married
	Infancy: being a "good" baby as culturally defined	Fussy or deformed child	Definitions around value of children

Source: Adapted from materials prepared by Dee Thornberry.

141

Social structures define life-stage tasks by generating social expectations. These expectations and their consequent social arrangements also have an impact on the person-environment transaction and require a careful analysis at each stage in the life cycle. Adults, for example, are generally expected to marry, and newly married couples are usually (at least in the dominant Anglo-American culture) expected to live separately from the parents of either partner. Social structures are developed to support these expectations, thereby creating resources for those whose behavior concurs with these expectations. Marriage customs, for example, provide social, psychological, and often monetary support to help young couples begin their married lives. The person who choses not to marry, or the person who establishes an intimate relationship with a same-sex partner, however, finds that the social-structural response often presents obstacles instead of resources. Stigmatization often replaces support. Again, it is import to keep human diversity in mind. Society itself is undergoing a transformation in terms of many of its expectations and somewhat more variation from the norm is tolerated than was true even a decade ago. These changes are the result of new migration patterns, demographic shifts, economic pressures, advances in biotechnology, and other factors.

Person-environment transactions are further influenced at each stage of the life cycle by culture. The values, beliefs, and expectations accompanying each stage of the life cycle are defined by culture. Social-structural arrangements usually reflect the values of the dominant culture. Cultural beliefs, for instance, lead to particular types of marriage ceremonies and customs, and for that matter determine that marriage is the appropriate task to accompany adulthood. Cultural beliefs, then, are resources in that they provide the value context for peoples' lives that is essential for them to develop a sense of identity and belonging. Minority cultures soon find, however, that when one's beliefs are at variance with those of the dominant culture, they become obstacles. The Spanish language, for instance, is a resource for Puerto Ricans in Puerto Rico, but may be experienced as an obstacle in those parts of the United States where Spanish is not commonly spoken.

We will now turn to an examination of specific stages in the life cycle and look at the resources and obstacles that either enhance or inhibit the accomplishment of the tasks accompanying each stage. The following stages will be used: conception and birth, infancy and childhood, adolescence, young adulthood, late adulthood, retirement, and death. Remember that the purpose of this analysis is to help you understand the person-environment transactions that are central to the professional task of making holistic assessments. It might be helpful for you to refer back to Figure 5.1 as you look at each stage. After examining the tasks confronting each stage of the life cycle, and looking at the related obstacles and resources, we will briefly discuss the implications for intervention and mention some of the roles assumed by professionals in the intervention process.

CONCEPTION AND BIRTH AS A LIFE STAGE

Tasks

Conception and birth is a period of expansion for individuals, groups, and society. For the individual (the parent), the self becomes the source of life for others. This generally adds to one's sense of competence, continuity, and importance, although it also increases one's responsibilities. For specific groups and for society as a whole, conception and birth ensure the survival of the social unit by replacing members and even increasing the size of the unit. The focus during this life stage is on decision making and preparation for new life. The decision to have a child is a significant one for the individuals directly involved. It engages a network of interpersonal relationships that will be used to provide emotional and financial support during the pregnancy and after the child is born. Groups impinge on individual decision making through cultural definitions of the desirability of pregnancy and the conditions under which it should occur. Groups also form the support structures that provide the context in which conception and birth occur.

Biological tasks focus on the reproductive act and the physical and emotional conditions needed for a healthy pregnancy and a secure birth. Psychological tasks relate to the readiness of the people involved to conceive and carry a child. This includes a sense of well-being about oneself and the baby, knowledge about conception, pregnancy, and birth, and the existence of emotional support systems. Social-structural tasks pertain to creating or finding an environment in which conception can occur by choice and the pregnancy and birth can occur in a safe context. Cultural tasks are those that engage belief and value systems to support the parents and the child. Together, these four task areas attempt to provide for the emotional and physical life-sustaining needs of the child and its parents. This includes the creation of a receptive social context in which the child will be able to grow and develop.

The life stage of conception and birth is unique in that, during it, the person being conceived and born is almost completely dependent on others. Conception itself is the result of decisions and actions by others which precede the person-to-be. The conditions under which the fetus develops are also strongly influenced by others, especially the biological parents. The task of the fetus itself—to develop physically and survive—is engaged through its genetically inherited developmental potential. Thus, for the fetus the task is almost exclusively physiological. The social, psychological, and cultural factors involved relate to the other people involved in the environment of the fetus. The biological mother is, of course, of particular importance. Even the birth process is heavily affected by others. The fetus has its own physiological tasks to perform in the birth process, but the environment into which the fetus emerges is determined by others. For example, even if a doctor diagnosed that a Caesarean section would be needed for a safe delivery, the parents would have to initiate the decisions and actions to make it possible.

This life stage is a good example of the fact that the tasks faced by individuals at various life-cycle stages affect each other. The task of the fetus is to grow and survive, though the likelihood of this happening is strongly influenced by the life-stage tasks of the biological parents. Are the parents unmarried adolescents or financially secure married adults? The readiness of biological parents to see a fetus through pregnancy, birth, and infancy is an important influence on the new person's ability to carry out his/her own life tasks. Although this point is easy to see at the life stage of conception and birth, it is true throughout the life cycle. In adulthood, the way in which one's sense of accomplishment and satisfaction develops (psychological tasks at that stage) is influenced by the way in which one's children have progressed through infancy, childhood, and adolescence, or the way one's own parents have handled the life tasks associated with retirement and death. Throughout the remainder of this chapter, the emphasis will be on the life tasks facing the individual encountering the life-cycle stage being discussed. Nevertheless, you should keep in mind the ways in which the interaction between life-cycle stages influences the performance of life tasks throughout the life cycle.

Resources

Biological resources are those which increase the probability that the mother and child will be healthy. These include the mother's age at conception, her previous pregnancy history, her health, and whether she is addicted to any substances. In general, women between the ages of about 16 and 35 run the least risk of complications during pregnancy. Women who are healthy—that is, who are disease-free and receive proper nutrition—who have not had pregnancy difficulties in the past, and who are not dependent on any drugs or narcotics are least likely to encounter biological difficulties during pregnancy. The age, nutritional level, and health of the father are also relevant to the biological processes of conception and pregnancy. Finally, the genetic composition of both parents is an important determinant of the course of a pregnancy and birth.

Psychological resources are those that help parents decide whether they wish to have a child and whether they have the emotional and financial means to do so. This includes knowledge about parenthood, conception, pregnancy, and birth—knowledge basic to informed decision making that will ultimately relate to one's sense of readiness for parenthood. Personality variables are also important. A sense of personal well-being and strength, and the ability to confront new situations help people adjust to the demands of pregnancy and parenthood. Willingness to share with others and the ability to cope effectively with physical and emotional stress are also helpful.

Social-structural resources are those factors that provide concrete help for pregnant women and new parents, as well as social-structural conditions that serve to validate one's changed identity as a parent. Tax benefits for children, health insurance to pay for the medical costs of pregnancy and birth, and employee policies that allow a woman to take leave during pregnancy are all significant resources. Additional social-structural resources include the quality of medical care available, social rituals such as baby showers that allow family and friends to indicate their support, the availability of information about conception and parenthood, and personal and genetic counseling. There is a direct relationship between minority group membership and the availability of these socioeconomic resources. Social-structural resources are generally more available to the non-poor, which usually means to members of the dominant groups.

Cultural resources are those that provide group approval for conception and birth and that provide a knowledge context for these activities. Being the proper age and having appropriate marital status as defined by one's own group places pregnancy in an acceptable value framework that will lead to social praise and support. Using socially acceptable means of prenatal care, following prescribed sex-role behaviors, and involving appropriate others, such as parents and siblings, are also common cultural beliefs and values that support conception, pregnancy, and birth. Of course, each cultural group has its own definitions of whether conception is desirable, and if so, how it should be managed.

Obstacles

As was shown in the earlier discussion of resources and obstacles, obstacles are those factors that increase the biological and psychological risks of conception and birth and detach people from the usual social-structural and cultural supports at this life stage. Biological obstacles would include a woman being very young or old at conception, or having a history of pregnancy complications. Other biological obstacles might include the presence of a venereal disease in either parent, substance abuse or dependency by the mother, or the existence of genetically transmitted problems in either parent. Psychological obstacles might be having to adjust to an unwanted child or very limited knowledge of conception, pregnancy, and birth. Another psychological obstacle would be feelings of severe inadequacy by either parent in terms of their new parenting responsibilities.

Examples of social-structural obstacles would be inadequate financial resources to pay for necessary medical treatment or to provide proper nutrition for the mother, abusive physical conditions that threaten the mother's biological and emotional well-being, and medical technology that is inadequate for the mother's needs (a factor that is especially important if there is a complication during pregancy or at birth). Additional social-structural obstacles would include lack of information about conception, pregnancy, and parenthood, and the unavailability of counseling to help parents who are struggling with factors related to conception. As noted earlier, poverty is directly related to physical well-being. Therefore, biological and social-structural resources/obstacles are closely associated, because poverty results from economic and political variables. Cultural obstacles are those beliefs and values that devalue conception and birth. Usually this occurs only for certain categories of people. For example, unmarried women may be considered unfit to bear children. Another example is when a dominant group denigrates conception among members of minority groups, such as when white Americans fear that black Americans have too many children. In both of these examples, obstacles discourage conception or make the conception, pregnancy, and birth processes more biologically or socially problematic.

Implications for Intervention

Conceiving a child is a major life event. For many it involves a decision that requires as much information and emotional support as possible. It is often a decision shared with significant others, such as family and friends, who can be critical elements in the decision. For some, conception is not decided, it simply happens. This often reflects lack of information about basic physiological processes. In other cases, conception is considered a natural part of life and accepted whenever it occurs. And for still others, it is a decision made to achieve other goals such as a sense of intimacy with another, a feeling of personal importance, or a feeling of independence. Professionals have to be able to disentangle the many factors that may be involved in conception in order to provide appropriate resources.

Pregnancy is a time of physical and emotional changes and adjustments. The pregnant woman needs as much information as possible about her pregnancy and a great deal of support as she adjusts her activities and emotions to it. Many women also need financial aid, housing, and other supports so that adequate nutrition and physical care are available. Others involved in the pregnancy, especially the father, also need to be supported and informed. When the pregnancy threatens to lead to exclusion from supporting social structures—such as school, family, work, and so on—efforts should be made to strengthen these linkages or find alternatives. The existence of conditions that threaten the physical well-being of the mother or child—such as drug addiction, disease, illness, or genetic factors—demands a thorough analysis of their implications so that appropriate action can be taken. When physically or psychologically needed and culturally acceptable, abortion is a resource that some may wish to consider.

The birth process is often approached with fear and uncertainty. This frequently reflects lack of information and fear of pain. It may also reflect anxiety over medical costs or disagreement with the medical procedures most commonly used in hospitals. Alternative places and methods of delivery should be explored in order to find those most compatible with a particular person's situation and background. Planning for the care of the newborn infant is also important, especially in cases where the mother may be alone, lack resources, be ill, or be ambivalent about her pregnancy.

There are a host of concerns that professionals can anticipate at this life stage. As we have seen, the needs for information, for physical and medical care, for help in decision making, and for solidifying linkages with support systems are especially critical. In addition, basic life-sustaining resources may be needed, such as money, food, and shelter. The fact that this life stage usually leads to alterations in established life patterns often creates the need for counseling in one or more of the multiple systems that may be involved. For many people, creating new life is a happy, exciting adventure. For others it is quite routine. Still others approach it with fear, anxiety, and a sense of desperation. Professionals must be able to anticipate and respond to all those possibilities so that the newly conceived person can have the best possible chance of meeting his/her basic task at this life stage—physical development and survival.

In summary, practice and policy issues are brought to bear at each stage of the life cycle. One of the primary concerns of the professional at the conception and birth stage (as with all other subsequent stages) is to identify potential obstacles as early as possible, and to provide resources to overcome them or at least minimize their impact. This may require the generalist practitioner to perform a variety of roles. Early identification of at-risk populations requires skills in case finding. After the populations are identified, special referral skills may be needed to get potential users to appropriate resources. Often, however, resources are not available, in which case skills are needed in mobilizing new resources. Another common problem is that resources may be there but barriers (such as rigid eligibility requirements) may inhibit their use. In this instance professionals need to develop skills in advocacy, both for the benefit of the individual potential user and for the entire population of users. Knowledge about the person-environment transactions at each stage of the life cycle, therefore, informs not only daily practice interventions but policy making as well.

INFANCY AND EARLY CHILDHOOD AS A LIFE STAGE

Tasks

As defined here, infancy and early childhood make up the period from birth to about 4 years of age. Infancy is a period that involves the infant as well as those around it, and so the tasks at this life stage reflect this range of people. Generally, infancy is a period of growth. The child gradually matures biologically, gaining more and more mastery over his/her own limbs, bodily functions, perceptual abilities, communication mechanisms, emotional states, and relationships with others. Part of these accomplishments occur through the development of language. The infant's parents also grow, responding to new demands on their time, energy, and emotions. Their relationship with each other—if there are two of them—is modified, as well as their interactions with other family members, friends, and social institutions. For the infant, then, the major task is to develop biologically, psychologically, and socially. For the parents the task is to find new life patterns and satisfactions through parenthood, and to protect and nurture the new member of society so it will grow into a productive participant in the social structure.

Resources

The biological resources of the infant are its genetic endowments. Capacities in the form of reflexes, brain characteristics, neurological mechanisms, skeletal structure, and basic organic health make it possible for the infant to gradually perceive, organize, and master its environment. The degree of development and mastery will, of course, reflect the nature of the child's genetic equipment. An infant's physical attractiveness, as defined culturally, is also an important biological resource. For the parents, biological resources would encompass their own physical well-being and their ability to perceive and handle the infant. Psychological resources in the infant are closely tied to biological endowments. However, the interaction between biological needs and the social environment is extremely important, with psychological resources emerging as a result. An infant whose needs are met consistently and promptly will usually develop personality resources that increase the probability of continued growth and strength. Social and physical stimulation will enable the infant to develop its perceptual and cognitive capacities, as well as its ability to relate happily to others. Parents' resources include their knowledge of parenting and infant development, their ability to adapt to the new demands imposed by the infant, and their sense of competence, which enables them to undertake the often difficult and uncertain activities involved in child-rearing.

Social-structural resources for the infant are those structures which enhance its survival and its growth efforts. The family— broadly defined, not just in terms of the intact family—is obviously of critical importance. The nature of the medical care available, neighborhood resources that relate to the adequacy of housing, nutrition, physical security, interpersonal relationships, and child care facilities are also examples of important social-structural resources. These resources are also important for the parents, although their resources might also include the availability of education about child-rearing, friendship networks, and access to socioeconomic resources. Culturally, the infant benefits from beliefs and values defining children as desirable and attractive, as well as those specifying that children should be cared for and not abused. For the parents, culture provides guidance as to how the infant should be reared and usually provides moral support for undertaking the child-rearing function.

Obstacles

For the infant, obstacles are those factors which impede growth and development. Given the infant's fragility, genetic and environmental obstacles can easily be life-threatening. For the parents, efforts to care for the infant can be blocked by a variety of obstacles. Biologically, the infant's genetic equipment may be incomplete or partially nonfunctional, making it more difficult for him/her to perform life-sustaining activities or interact with the environment so that growth and development occur. This would be the case for infants born without an organ or a limb; with a defective organ, such as the heart; or with brain damage. An infant who contracted a disease would also be placed at risk. An unusual or undesirable physical appearance can also be an obstacle, for example a cleft palate, crossed eyes, or a limb deformity. Parents may also encounter biological obstacles. The blind or deaf parent, for instance, has a much more difficult job relating to the child in order to perceive and meet its needs.

For the child, psychological obstacles are closely related to its biological capacity to perceive and organize the environment and to process information cognitively. The development of fearful or rigid personality responses to stimuli may also be obstacles to continued growth. These chronic distress responses can also precipitate unhelpful behaviors by others. Parents' personality patterns can be obstacles when they lead to compulsive activities toward the infant that restrict rather than enhance its growth.

Social-structural obstacles for the child may include inadequacies of nutrition, physical care, and nurturance that result from poverty, family structures that cannot sustain child-rearing activities, disorganized communities, and parents who have not had the opportunity to learn how to parent. These factors also operate as obstacles for parents. Cultural obstacles include beliefs and values that denigrate certain types of infants, such as the deformed, the illegitimate, the "fussy," and prejudices toward minority and ethnic groups. Cultural practices can also be obstacles when they mandate child care practices that conflict with biological needs; for example, excessively early toilet training. For parents who are members of certain groups, cultural values and beliefs that preach that they cannot or should not rear children are obstacles. In the United States, this applies to single parents, homosexuals, and the physically handicapped, among others. Members of these groups can and do successfully care for infants, but they have to fight dominant cultural values and beliefs representing them as incompetent.

Implications for Intervention

Infants need a great deal of care if they are to thrive and develop. This requires many resources, including knowledge, money, energy, love, food, shelter, and time. Many parents may lack these resources, and the support systems available to them may be similarly depleted. Professionals need to be able to assess the resources available, always taking into account the child-rearing strategies appropriate to a person's cultural environment.

The infant may also need help. A child born with a genetic limitation or who suffers a severe illness needs careful diagnostic and treatment resources. Parents and others may need financial help to pay for these services, as well as knowledge and emotional support to be able to use them most effectively. An infant needing special care often imposes substantial strains on the whole family system, and the resulting needs have to be addressed by the practitioner. Relationships between the infant and the parents can also be affected.

In the American myth, the infant is enshrined in a cradle of affluence and acceptance. However, this myth does not always agree with reality. Babies are sometimes burdens on already strained financial, emotional, or time resources. When they require special care they can be even more disruptive. Understanding the joys as well as the heartaches of infancy as a life stage for infants and parents alike requires careful analysis and sensitivity.

The period of infancy and early childhood is a time of rapid growth and development involving physical, psychomotor, and affective changes in the child. During this period the child gains an increasing sense of mastery over the environment, and, if normative patterns follow, acquires one of the most powerful of all human tools—language. The repertoire of professional tasks bearing on this life-cycle stage involves both macro (social policy) and micro (direct service) roles. Social policy efforts need to assure that the social-structural supports such as sufficient income, proper nutrition, adequate housing, and access to health care are available for both the child and the caregiver. Prevention of problems, restoration of lost or impaired functioning, and provision of ongoing supportive services are all ways in which person-environment transactions are affected by policy and practice.

MIDDLE AND LATE CHILDHOOD AS A LIFE STAGE

Tasks

Middle and late childhood is defined here as the period from approximately age 4 to 12. It is a period during which biological development continues to be very important but comes to be shaped more and more by social interaction in an increasingly wide range of social situations. Childhood tasks are to continue the biological growth and development necessary for healthy organic functioning, as well as to lay the foundation for life-long personality characteristics and cognitive functioning. Physical health, personality strength and adaptability, and cognitive capacity form the foundation for life-long participation as a member of society. The tasks of childhood, then, serve individual growth needs as well as society's efforts to socialize people to become responsible participants in the social system.

Resources

Biological resources available to children are similar to those available to infants, so they need not be discussed further here. Sometimes, though, it is only when a child begins school and interacts with a wider range of people than those in his/her family that particular biological resources are noted. This could include unusually well developed coordination, muscle strength, hearing, and eyesight, and overall resistance to disease. Psychological resources also continue to develop from infancy, but they are especially important in childhood. Substantial cognitive development occurs in school and through modeling the behavior of peers, family members, and media personalities. The child endowed genetically with high intelligence, sound perceptual organs, and general health enabling these genetic endowments to be fully developed has important biological/psychological resources for his/her use in confronting childhood tasks. Psychological development, including the development of intelligence, is also strongly related to social experiences, as will be discussed further. Continued physical and social stimulation that confronts children with challenging but manageable stresses helps them develop a sense of competence and well-being. Continued parental nurturance and support also facilitate the development of a stable self-identity that can adapt to increasingly diversified and new life experiences.

Social-structural resources continue to be important to a person's development from infancy through childhood. Family structure, community environment, school systems, and friendship networks are extremely important sources of opportunities for the child to encounter new people and situations. When these structures support the child's biological growth and psychological development they become extremely powerful resources. For example, parents who are supportive of exploratory activities by the child and who gently cushion occasional failures help make the world seem a rich and exciting place. Schools that stimulate cognitive and social development by presenting manageable challenges in a structured but supportive context also encourage a sense of security through growth. Cultural values can be resources when they mandate respect for children's needs and involvement of children in the full range of life activities. For example, in knowing their grandparents children are exposed to cross-generational learning that they might otherwise miss, and children who participate appropriately in adult activities are better prepared to perform them when they are adults themselves.

Obstacles

Biological obstacles in infancy often become increasingly limiting as the child grows and is exposed to increased demands. The malnourished child may find it difficult to play with friends or to concentrate in school. The child with limited physical mobility may become increasingly isolated from his/her active peers. Sometimes biological obstacles only become apparent in childhood. Hearing or vision impairment are examples of deficits that are sometimes identified for the first time in school. Biological obstacles become increasingly enmeshed in a web of relationships with social structures, and their ultimate significance in a child's life will depend on how these relationships are developed. The child with cerebral palsy who is seen as an embarrassment will not receive needed therapy and will gradually become weaker and less mobile. The child with an uncorrected vision deficit will find school a frustrating, boring experience and may act out as a result. Even a child who has to wear glasses may be ridiculed by peers and gradually withdraw socially. Mitigating these effects of obstacles requires careful medical diagnosis and supportive relationships.

Psychological obstacles are frequently tied to biological ones— although they also reflect social obstacles, as we will see. The child with cognitive limitations or perceptual deficits may find demands by others difficult to understand and impossible to fullfill. Even psychological and biological resources can be overwhelmed by excessive or harsh demands that generate fear, anxiety, with-drawal, and rigidity. If the world is seen as cruel, unmanageable, and threatening, then the child's psychological development is likely to be restricted. This will lessen the child's ability to understand and adapt flexibly and productively to situations. The reasons the environment seems so hostile may be biological, social, or cultural, but the results are similar regardless of their source. Therefore, we can expect that a child of average intelli-gence who is regularly pushed into educational and social situations beyond his/her abilities will react with hostility, anxiety, and withdrawal. Of course, the amount of interpersonal support the child receives will influence the kind of personality that ultimately develops.

Social-structural obstacles can be many for the child. Any structured social events that reduce the child's sense of safety, security, competence, mastery, or health become obstacles. The sources of such events can be many: poverty (chronic ill health, hunger, anxiety over physical safety); racism or other forms of prejudice and discrimination (physical assaults, attacks on one's identity and personal integrity); natural disasters; accidents; unhealthy family structures (child abuse, either physical or mental); unhealthy school structures (rigid, overly demanding, non-supportive situations); and even peer groups that scapegoat a child. Because the child moves into an increasingly broad range of social situations, its contact with social-structural resources and obstacles is greatly increased over that of the infant. Cultural obstacles are those values and beliefs that inhibit the child's development. Excessive protectiveness can be a great cultural obstacle, as can beliefs that ignore the child's need for privacy, play, protection, and nurturing.

Implications for Intervention

Childhood is the critical beginning of a person's interactions with a complex environment. These interactions are an important part of growth, but they can easily become overwhelming and restricting. For some children, the environment may be too unstructured or too lacking in interaction opportunities to provide the challenges necessary for growth. For others, the environment may be too structured and demanding. Professionals need to be able to assess the ways in which existing environments are able to respond to a child's efforts to understand, adapt, and grow. Sometimes environments need to be enriched, other times they need to be simplified. In all cases, the focus is on helping the child find the resources needed in a particular environment— whether those resources be family activities, available life-sustaining resources, or school-system activities.

There is considerable agreement among theorists that child-hood is a time when the basic personality is established. Although it is subject to modification throughout life, a view of the world as essentially benign or fearsome seems to be established by the end of childhood. At this life stage, then, the interaction between the individual and the environment is especially critical. Adults frequently have enough knowledge and power to modify the child's environment if they feel the need to do so, but the child has relatively little power to do this. Thus, it is the job of professionals as well as parents to focus on making the environment as supportive as possible for the child's efforts to grow and develop both biologically and socially.

A variety of social welfare services are available to prevent and alleviate some of the problems frequently occurring during the developmental stages of middle and late childhood. These include such child welfare services as residential child care facilities, foster homes, child health programs, income maintenance services, recreational programs, and supportive services such as day care centers. Again, it is important to keep in mind the concept of reciprocity. Parents, too, may be dealing with their own develop-mental crises. Some of the abuse and neglect problems that social workers commonly deal with may be rooted in the clash between the developmental needs of children and those of their parents.

ADOLESCENCE AS A LIFE STAGE

Tasks

The major tasks of adolescence, defined here as approximately age 13 to 18, revolve around biological development and further integration into social institutions. Adolescence is characterized by somewhat selective biological developments. Basic motor, perceptual, and cognitive maturation has already occurred in infancy and childhood. In adolescence there is generally a substantial increase in physical size, height, and weight. Sexual maturation also occurs, including the emergence of secondary sex characteristics, such as breast development, growth of body hair, and so on. The rapid growth in size and sexual maturation that occurs involves substantial hormonal changes that can affect physical appearance and emotional needs. A large part of the adolescent's task, then, is to adjust to changes in body image, physical capacities, and sexual needs.

These biological changes take place within a social context that is also changing. School demands are more academically rigorous and are increasingly related to lifelong planning. For example, academic success affects whether one goes to college and, in turn, future career opportunities. School also becomes an increasingly important social arena in which peer-group pressure accelerates. Lifelong friendships and interaction patterns can be established at this time. Biological development, academic demands, and peer pressure naturally intersect. The adolescent confronts a changing self, making it difficult to understand precisely what his/her needs and capabilities are. The friendship patterns that character- ized childhood may suddenly seem inappropriate as young people struggle to find acceptance among their peers. Intellectual capacity, physical skill, and physical appearance are dimensions that heavily influence the kinds of social demands and oppor- tunities available to an adolescent. This is further affected by the child's race, ethnicity, and sex. For example, a young woman who matures and grows in size early in her adolescence may feel awkward and sexually vulnerable, while one who experiences these events later may be more ready to integrate them into her social relationships with others. The reverse is true for young men, who tend to grow and mature later than women. But the young man whose development is late even for his gender often comes to feel weak and unattractive.

Naturally, the support adolescents get from others is critical to their development. This can be problematic for parents who experience anxiety over the increasing size, competence, de- mands, and autonomy of their children. Rather than assisting their children's development, they may try to maintain their parental control by denying the adolescent's new-found com- petence or by emphasizing the significance of biological changes in order to increase the young person's sense of uncertainty and hence his/her need for parental protection. Other adults, espe- cially teachers, can also reinforce either the youngster's sense of developing strength and well-being or his/her awkwardness and anxiety. From society's point of view, adolescence is a time of some normative flexibility, so that biological changes and the erratic approaches to need-meeting they sometimes create can be accommodated. Yet society still expects that by the end of adolescence the developing adult will be ready to assume a relatively stable role as an adult in the social order.

Resources

As suggested above, the adolescent's physical resources are often prodigious. Physical strength and size are powerful resources, as are the continued strengthening of perceptual and cognitive abilities. Adequate nutrition is an important resource during this period. Sexual functioning matures during adolescence—itself a powerful motivator for behavior. Psychologically, adolescents bring their biological abilities to bear on establishing enduring patterns of relationships with their peers and with adults. These become important beginnings of support systems that will continue throughout life. Perceptual and cognitive resources are especially important for meeting increasing societal demands for achievement in an expanding range of areas— among which school, work, and family are especially important. Through this process, the personality is gradually enriched by increasing mutuality in relationships, deepening of interests, and a clearer articulation of personal values and goals.

Social-structural rescources are those which promote the adolescent's sense of competence and need for individuation. The family continues to be an important potential source of support, and the peer group assumes increased importance as an influence on behavior. School becomes a potential source of enrichment, while the youngster's increased size and physical and mental capacities enable him/her to participate in a wider range of institutional activities, such as driving, working, church-related groups, school-sponsored trips and activities, and so on. Culturally, values become very important resources, helping adolescents solidify their self-identity and self-image as well as order personal values and lifelong priorities. Decisions about the balance between work and family, self and others, achievements and sharing, and stability and change grow out of cultural values.

Obstacles

Biological development can be an obstacle in a variety of ways during adolescence. The biological changes that occur may not be well understood and may therefore create social difficulties. The young person's body development is a case in point. Changes in size and strength can create appearance and behavior character-istics that are denigrated by others—the very tall young woman, or the overly enthusiastic and slightly uncontrolled and uncoor-dinated young man are two instances of adolescents who receive such treatment. Illness and accidents are also possible when physical growth is not supported by adequate nutrition, or when growth between the various parts of the body is not synchronous. Hormonal changes are common and can create fairly rapid and extensive fluctuations in energy levels, moods, and sense of well-being. Physical and psychological changes are closely related, because for the adolescent the emerging adult body is a critical component of self-image and treatment by others. Developmental irregularities or problems often bring ridicule and isolation during adolescence, which in turn can have powerful effects on feelings of competence and well-being. This is especially true if childhood experiences have begun the process of accentuating weaknesses rather than strengths. However, perceptual and cognitive capacities can be used to mitigate the negative psycho-logical effects of physical obstacles. The very intelligent woman, for example, may be treated with respect even though she may not be pretty by conventional definitions.

Social-structural obstacles limit development by restricting access to resources or creating social expectations that are inhibiting. Poor adolescents may lack proper nutrition or may need medical care to deal with myopia (near-sightedness), a biological condition that often accompanies the rapid growth that occurs during adolescence. Families may have unrealistic social or academic expectations for their children, and thus push them into situations in which success is practically impossible. Schools sometimes emphasize young people's weaknesses, which may then create or reinforce peer-group difficulties. The peer group itself can be an extremely damaging obstacle as it forces young people to conform to stereotyped expectations regarding dress, behavior, and interpersonal relationships. Cultural values can further exacerbate social-structural obstacles by legitimating disadvantaging expectations. For instance, bright women are hurt by cultural values that restrict women to the home, and physically limited men are denigrated by values that emphasize large physical size and strength. Because socialization is such an important part of the adolescent's developing and maturing sense of self, cultural values can greatly shape—and inhibit—personal growth and development.

Implications for Intervention

During any type of change, either personal or social, people are put at a risk. Therefore, their efforts to understand and find appropriate responses to changes need to be strongly supported. Otherwise, the uncertainties accompanying change can gradually erode the individual's sense of competence. Supporting people through change entails providing information, emotional resources, and help in keeping the pieces of shifting institutional relationships in balance. For example, practitioners often help adolescents manage relationships between their emerging sexuality, their desire for rewarding interpersonal relationships, increasing autonomy at home, and school demands. In doing this, of course, many people have to be involved besides the particular adolescent.

Professionals are also heavily involved with modifying social expectations for adolescents. Although there is some flexibility built into the role of adolescent, there are many inconsistencies and strains in role definitions. For example, men are generally allowed to be more sexually promiscuous than are women. Therefore, some groups of adolescents—in the United States, females—may be punished for behavior permissible for others. Professionals attempt to make social expectations more equitable, and when adolescents are punished, to protect their needs for support and care—preventing their acquiring prison records if possible, keeping them from being expelled from school, avoiding unnecessary estrangement from their families, and so on. Often the family is a major source of difficulty in the development of appropriate perceptions of and responses to the needs of adolescents, explaining in part why social workers so often work with families. Adolescents can sometimes appear gawky, homely, and unlovable as they struggle to understand their own bodies and function effectively in the world around them. It is important to try and help the individual adolescent and society—family, teachers, peers, and so on—approach each other with greater awareness, caring, and support.

The emotional turbulence of adolescence may precipitate a resurgence of unresolved conflicts in caregivers (recall the concept of reciprocity), many of whom are attempting to deal with the transitional crises of midlife. They need to be helped to distinquish between activities that are focused on achieving their own goals, and those that are needed by their adolescent children. A number of social welfare services exist to help adolescents and those with whom they interact. These include: vocational and educational counseling; corrections; alcohol and chemical dependency counseling; and a wide range of supportive, educational, recreational, and psychotherapeutic services. These programs and services share the goal of assisting the adolescent to successfully accomplish the tasks confronting this often-difficult life stage.

ADULTHOOD AS A LIFE STAGE

Tasks

Adulthood can be divided into three major periods: young adulthood, roughly from 18 to 25 years of age; middle adulthood, from approximately 25 to 45; and late adulthood, from 45 to 61. Although each period has somewhat distinctive tasks, resources, and obstacles, for the purposes of this book we can talk about adulthood as a whole. Readers are encouraged to think and study on their own about the three subparts. Adulthood is a time of accomplishment and productivity—probably the period when people are the most goal-directed with respect to their own life aspirations. However, society expects that individual aspirations will mesh with societal needs. For example, rearing children requires resources that are earned—and spent—through the economic system. Socialization in childhood and adolescence is the major mechanism through which adults are prepared to work toward their goals in socially acceptable ways. Individual goals and societal goals, then, are assumed to come together during adulthood. At no other life stage is the individual quite so oriented toward the performance of societal tasks. Naturally, members of diverse groups process societal goals and means of achieving them through their own particular values, resources, and obstacles.

In addition to working toward the attainment of task goals, adulthood is a time when one seeks interpersonal intimacy, and when enduring relationships with others are formed, some of which generally include sexual activity. Marriage is, of course, one pattern, but others include parenting relationships, non-married coupling, and selected friendships. The adult's sense of accomplishment and well-being are, for most people, heavily dependent on the formation of close interpersonal relationships that provide important social, biological, and psychological supports. Although adulthood is a period of autonomous goal-seeking behavior carried out in the major institutions of society, it is also a time of personal nurturance through the special relationships found in adulthood—marriage or other forms of coupling, parenting, and so on. Thus, in a sense, adulthood is both outwardly and inwardly focused; a time of both independence and interdependence.

Resources

In adulthood, people usually have as many physical resources as they will ever have. Although physical development continues, gradually moving into increasingly degenerative conditions, adulthood is generally characterized by well-developed physical, perceptual, cognitive, and psychological resources. Levels of development vary, of course, but cannot be substantially changed in adulthood. Their use can vary, however. Use is a function of social-structural variables which either facilitate or inhibit adult behavior.

Social-structural resources for adults are found primarily in the major institutions of society that serve to organize people's behavior around the performance of significant life tasks. Through the family and family-like structures, adults solidify their most intimate interpersonal relationships. The economic institution is an important arena in which people achieve their task-oriented goals, although women have also traditionally achieved many task goals through their child-rearing activities in the family. The political institution interacts extensively with the economic institution and also provides opportunities for significant decision making. The educational, religious, and social welfare institutions may also support task-oriented activities. Inevitably, the interactions between adults and social institutions vary for different types of adults. Although the institutional structures support the goal-directed behavior of most adults of the dominant group, we saw in an earlier chapter that it may affect other adults quite differently. Cultural values support adults' efforts to be independent in most of their interpersonal behaviors. However, we will see below that independence is not always functional, and that dominant cultural values in the United States tend to arbitrarily limit the range of socially acceptable interpersonal behaviors.

Obstacles

Although illness and accidents can occur at any point in the life cycle, higher rates of both begin to characterize middle and late adulthood. This reflects the stresses that accompany adult life tasks, as well as the range of behaviors in which adults engage. For example, work-related accidents and illnesses occur primarily in adulthood, because it spans the major working years. Also, a great deal of violence occurs in the context of the family, especially between adults. Even the degenerative processes of the physical organism accelerate, most commonly in the areas of vision, hearing, strength, and quickness of cognitive processes. These changes are not usually substantial enough to have a major effect on behavior during adulthood, but their influence does grow cumulatively.

A major potential obstacle in adulthood is sometimes the gradual deterioration of personality adaptiveness. This may result in part from physical changes that are perceived as modifying appearance and behavior in undesirable ways. Even such relatively unimportant biological changes as loss or graying of hair or changes in skin texture can generate anxiety and defensiveness. Adults sometimes deny these physical changes by using cosmetics, wearing different clothes, or even associating with younger, more "attractive" people. This can have seriously disruptive consequences for long-established and important supportive relationships with spouses, mates, siblings, close friends, and others. The loss of these supports can undermine the individual's personality resources and lead to depression or other types of alienation and isolation.

A second assault on psychological functioning in adulthood results from the interplay of social-structural and personality variables. Adulthood is, as has been noted, the principal period in the life cycle when cherished life goals are sought through such activities as work, peer relationships, family or family-like relationships, and so on. However, it is only in rare cases that all of an individual's life goals are attained, and during adulthood the individual has to begin to come to terms with this reality. Social-structural resources naturally play a significant role in an individual's ability to achieve life goals. Poverty, destructive family or family-like relationships, unemployment, accidents or injuries, and the loss of loved ones can all block goal attainment. When this occurs, the individual's own sense of identity and self-worth are called into question. Even worse, there seems less and less time left in life to try again. The sense of personal and societal failure is further exacerbated by dominant cultural values stressing success—especially financial success—and achievement. Psychological responses can include a whole range of defensive actions, sometimes even changing the place in which one lives so that the failure will not be so apparent. Cultural values may also inhibit the efforts of diverse groups to meet the needs of their adult members. For example, some homosexuals are pressured into loveless heterosexual marriages and furtive homosexual contacts, while many women accept physical and emotional abuse rather than endure the stigma of divorce—even today when divorce is much more common than in the past.

Implications for Intervention

Adulthood is a long and complex life stage, encompassing the period of life when firm commitments are made to people and tasks. These, of course, are modified and renegotiated as time goes on and as people adjust to the changing relationship between their goals and accomplishments. This may, for example, include divorce and remarriage (or similar events for non-married couples) and job or career changes. Energy also changes, so that the motivation of earlier stages of adulthood may gradually disappear over time. Yet, if there is such a phenomenon as overall satisfaction with one's life, its roots are in adulthood—the time of life when goals are formulated and when the most significant efforts are made to achieve them. If these goals are substantially achieved, life is usually seen as happy; if not, the future may look bleak indeed.

Obviously, adulthood is a time of excitement, challenge, and stress. Practitioners need to be prepared to support people and to help them cope with such stresses of adult life as work pressure, relationship problems, and parenting demands. It is also critical that the social structure reward people's plans and activities. Institutionalized discrimination, for instance, systematically blocks the efforts of certain groups to achieve their goals. In offering help, professionals need to recognize that adults are a very special group with which to work. They often strongly value their independence and autonomy, as cultural values have taught them to do. They frequently resist offers of help from others, even professionals. A sense of competence is extremely important for adults, and one must exercise the utmost care in supporting and preserving it. At the same time, adulthood is a time of stress and challenge during which personal support and institutional intervention are frequently needed.

Recalling the concept of reciprocity, it should be clear that people rarely live in isolation from others. Pinpointing the social services focusing exclusively on adulthood as a developmental stage, therefore, is difficult. Family-centered social services assist in the resolution of many of the stage-specific problems that tend to surface during this period of individual and family development. Rhodes (1977) conceptualizes the family as an ecological system that progresses through courtship, childbearing and rearing, and post-parental stages. Each stage, according to Rhodes, demands qualitatively different adaptations. Based on Erikson's stages of individual life cycles, Rhodes identifies two themes that characterize adulthood: companionship versus isolation, and regrouping versus binding or expulsion. Major changes in family relationships occur as teenagers increasingly meet emotional needs outside the family. Parents, who have often set aside their companionship needs to meet the challenge of parenting, may find their relationship with one another revitalized. Regrouping versus binding or expulsion applies to the stage in which children leave their parental home to establish new families. According to Rhodes, the essential task at this developmental stage is allowing for the separation of the children as a natural result of their growth and maturity. The ability to accomplish this task rests heavily on developing a strong marital relationship separate from the parenting function.

Increasingly, however, adults are choosing alternatives to the traditional nuclear family pattern. Remaining single, developing an intimate relationship with a same-sex partner, and having a childless marriage are choices more and more people are making. These emerging patterns bring new life-stage demands for which there are few role models.

Exhibit 5.1 at the end of this chapter focuses on one commonly discussed issue of adulthood as a life stage—the midlife transitional crisis as it relates to males. Although the exhibit is instructive in terms of raising important issues, once again human diversity variables need to be underlined. Gilligan (1982) questions the applicability of a male-dominated life-cycle theory to the experience of women, and points out that women bring to the life cycle a different viewpoint, different priorities, and an alternative perspective on maturity. The hallmark of this perspective, according to Gilligan, is a moral understanding based on a greater orientation toward the value of supportive relationships and useful networks of interdependence.

RETIREMENT AS A LIFE STAGE

Tasks

Retirement, defined here as the period from approximately age 62 to death, is a period of adjustment to loss. Exhibit 5.2 at the end of the chapter, however, raises important questions about what the retirement age should be. It is a time when biological capacities continue to degenerate, when many productive roles—especially the roles of work and parenting—are left behind, and when significant others in one's life are lost through death. Retirement also involves planning for reduced earning capacity, changed living arrangements, and increased health care needs. And, as importantly as any other life task, retirement entails preparing for death. Obviously this life stage is one of tremendous change and adjustment, both biologically and socially. Indeed, these two areas interact closely, and the nature of their interaction is the major determinant of whether retirement is a time of contentment or desperation. On the other hand, retirement is also a time of freedom from many of the tasks of earlier life stages, such as work, interpersonal responsibilities, and child-rearing. This allows more opportunity to engage in quiet contemplation and personally rewarding actitvities than is usually possible when one is younger and under more pressure. Many older people continue to live active professional lives. For them, old age is neither a period of retirement nor of disengagement from significant social roles.

Resources

Although old age entails physical deterioration in a number of areas, most older people continue to have relatively good health and retain most of their earlier perceptual and cognitive capacities until very advanced old age. Age itself, therefore, can be a resource. Of course, people age differently just as they differ in so many other ways, and some people experience advanced physical deterioration at relatively young ages. Nevertheless, most people are able to carry on their usual physical activities during retirement with relatively minor adjustments. Physical energy is used differently, however. Some older people tend to avoid the hectic pace younger people prefer and think their actions through more carefully before initiating them. In this sense, the elderly become more efficient, reflecting once again the strong tie between physical and psychological resources. Looking back on a lifetime of accomplishments, most older people find self-validation and satisfaction, and can adjust to lower energy levels by focusing on what is meaningful to them rather than on what society expects. To others, old age is a time of continued social and political activity, and a reference to this life stage as "the golden years" might indeed be offensive to them.

The relatively recent organization of older people into vocal pressure groups, such as the Gray Panthers, has helped strengthen social-structural resources for the elderly. A variety of financial aid programs exist to help maintain income in old age, as well as other concrete support services such as housing and transportation subsidies, in-home and congregate meal programs, and medical care services. More of these services are needed, however, especially for some groups of elderly people. Additional social needs are increasingly being recognized and met through self-help groups, the development of recreational programs, the creation of educational opportunities, and the provision of personal counseling services. There is a special emphasis now on structuring institutional arrangements so that older people can retain control over their own lives. Some of the arrangements currently being developed are housing that builds in both autonomy and immediate access to help, transportation systems that are more physically and financially accessible to the elderly, and counseling and financial supports to help link the older person to some type of family or family-like network. There is little doubt that existing social-structural arrangements sometimes impinge on the quality of life of older persons.

Cultural values have become extremely important determinants of the nature of retirement, and the self-help groups organized among older persons have had a noticeable impact. When the extended family is a common social-structural form, older people are usually taken care of primarily within the family unit. This is much less common in the nuclear family. However, other values also affect the treatment of the elderly. In a society that values autonomy and productivity, the elderly may not want to be limited by the roles to which they are relegated within the family. They may prefer to be socially and sexually active even if the primary spouse or mate dies, leading to the formation of new families and family-like units among older persons. They may also wish to define for themselves the extent of their involvement with children, grandchildren, and the economic system, rather than automatically assuming roles expected of them within their initial families of procreation. All of these structural changes reflect cultural values that are gradually changing to accommodate a much greater degree of independence and variation in the behavior of the elderly.

Obstacles

Even for the relatively healthy older person, increasing old age brings greater risks of illness, accidents, and physical deterioration. This may progressively limit the person's physical mobility and social participation. It may also strain the financial resources available to the older person. Gradually, the individual becomes more dependent on others. This can threaten his/her sense of self-identity and well-being. Combined with a commonly experienced gradual loss of perceptual acuity—especially sight, hearing, and taste—the older person may withdraw and become increasingly isolated. This often reduces the motivation for living, which can manifest itself in reduced food intake to the point of malnutrition, and a lack of mobility and stimulation that accelerates physical deterioration.

While there has been greatly increased recognition of the needs of the elderly in recent decades, social-structural factors still make retirement problematic. Young people grow up detached from older people and have not learned how to prepare for this life stage. When grown children move out of the home (sometimes called the "empty nest" syndrome) and when the worker has to retire, the abrupt loss of social roles leaves people feeling useless and undirected. The high cost of medical care creates anxieties that old age will lead to destitution. These conditions are perpetuated by cultural values that overemphasize youth and physical appearance, as well as productivity and independence. American society values progress and change and is always pushing toward the new with little respect for its own past or those who created it. In such a milieu, it is little wonder that older people feel left behind and left out. We know only too well that these feelings are closely tied to accelerated biological deterioration, social isolation, and psychological distress. Unfortunately, these are realities for many of the elderly. Many of these realities are reversible, however, and as the aged gain in political power, societal resources may be reallocated to more adequately meet the needs of this life-cycle stage.

Implications for Intervention

Like any type of diversity, old age has its particular resources and obstacles. Society holds conflicting views about the elderly. On one hand, it assumes that older people are physically and emotionally dependent; on the other hand, it tries to find ways to make them more self-sufficient, because they constitute a growing percentage of the population. Professionals,as part of their commitment to help people live self-directed lives, must reinforce societal efforts to recognize and support the many strengths of older people. For example, there is a need for many more apartment complexes that allow the elderly to live autonomously and still have access to immediate physical help and social companionship. There is also a need for nursing homes in which the older person's right to and need for privacy—including the privacy to express sexuality—is respected. Many other services are needed as well.

At the interpersonal level, we must be sensitive to older people's continuing need for friendship, social recognition, and intimate ties to others. An older person may need emotional support to adjust to a radically altered physical appearance or decreased physical mobility. A strong sense of self-respect is as important in retirement as it is at any other point in the life cycle. Help in meeting daily living needs is also sometimes of critical importance. This could include help in such diverse activities as securing transportation to health care facilities, applying for financial assistance, or selecting a nursing home.

DEATH AS A LIFE STAGE

Throughout this chapter we have been trying to persent a framework usable for analyzing human behavior in its social context at any point in the life cycle. The first part of the chapter described the framework itself. This was followed by the use of the framework to analyze the following life stages: conception and birth, infancy, childhood, adolescence, adulthood, and retirement. Now we would like to give you the opportunity to use the framework yourself to analyze death as a life stage. Hopefully, this will increase your mastery of the concept, as well as increasing your sense of confidence in its use. To assist you, we have provided some general guidelines below.

Before moving to the analytical framework, it will probably be helpful to stop and think for a minute about your own attitudes toward death. Young people are frequently shielded from death as a part of life: hospitals usually do not allow them to visit patients until they are adolescents, they are not taken to funerals, and they have very little contact with the elderly. When something is unfamiliar it often seems strange and even frightening. Many readers may feel this way about death. Yet today there is a rich literature about death and dying that can help one to better understand this part of the life cycle (see this chapter's references and additional readings for specific titles). As a professional, you will need to feel comfortable practicing in situations that include death or dying—when working in a hospital, for example. We have already seen that human life and social structures are characterized by diversity—a fact that professional helpers must learn to understand and appreciate. Death and dying is another element of this diversity. As you use the framework to analyze death as part of the life cycle, remind yourself that it is as important, as complex, and as fascinating as any other life-cycle stage. You will also need to understand and deal with death and dying as a professional, regardless of your personal feelings about their meaning in your own life.

Tasks

Think about the life tasks with which the individual and society are faced at death. What does each gain and what does each lose? One way to think this through is to try to imagine what would happen if people lived forever. What problems would be created that death helps solve? Another thing to think about is why people fear death—what they are really afraid of, and how does understanding their fear help one understand the life tasks to be accomplished at death? And, by the way, does thinking about death in terms of life tasks make it easier or more difficult for you to think about your own death?

Resources

Using the biological/psychological/social-structural/cultural format, determine what resources people have as they try to carry out the life tasks associated with death. Another way to think about this is in terms of those factors that make it easier for people to die. These might be biological factors, such as drugs; psychological factors, such as emotional security; social-structural factors, such as legal procedures to pass on resources to others; and cultural factors, such as beliefs about an afterlife and rituals to help people prepare for death. Resources, then, are the things that support people's efforts to die in such a way as to maximize their sense of personal and social well-being. Does it seem a contradiction to think of well-being at the point of death? Why or why not?

Obstacles

The opposite side of the resource coin would be the biological/ psychological/social-structural/cultural factors that make it more difficult for people to die. Think about pain, for example. Is it a resource, making it easier to die, or an obstacle, making it harder, or both? In thinking about obstacles, be sure to include relationships with others. When do relationships make it more difficult to die? When do they make it easier? Do you have difficulty thinking about obstacles, especially in relation to death? Why is this a painful subject for you, or why isn't it?

Implications for Interventions

To what aspects of dying should professionals be especially sensitive? Remember to think systematically so that you do not overlook help that those associated with the dying person might need, as well as help for the particular dying person. As you think about it, are there resources one might need in order to work effectively in the highly emotional situations in which death often occurs? What might these be, and would they include structural supports as well as personal resources? Could you work with someone in the last life-cycle stage? Think carefully about the problems you would anticipate if such a situation were part of your work responsibilities. How does such thinking help you understand the implications of death as a life stage for the helping professions?

SUMMARY

It is apparent that the life cycle encompasses a relentless progression of changes: some from within the organism itself and others generated by the external human and physical environment. Yet amid these changes there are some constants. These include certain lifelong tasks; namely, physical survival, physical development within the limits set by one's genetic inheritance, attempts to relate to others, developing and strengthening a sense of self-worth and competence, and task-focused behavior. We have seen how these constants are shaped somewhat differently at each life stage, and how the basic tasks remain constant nevertheless. Each life stage then adds its own particular tasks. Using the life cycle to understand behavior thus leads back to two important points made much earlier in this book: One is that human behavior involves the interaction between people and their environments. The second is that human beings have common human needs that are elaborated and met in extraordinarily diverse ways. The next and last chapter will examine further some implications of these two points.

STUDY QUESTIONS

1. Use the framework presented in Table 5.1 to analyze yourself at the life stage in which you now are. First, of course, identify the life stage and explain why you feel it is your current life-cycle stage. After doing your own analysis, go back to the chapter's dicussion of your life stage. Based on your analysis, do

you feel the chapter has omitted, overemphasized, or under-emphasized any aspect of the life stage? Discuss what you feel should be added or subtracted and why.

2. Now do the same type of analysis for someone you know well who is in a different life stage. A grandparent or younger sibling would be possible choices. Be sure to identify the life stage, analyze it, and compare your analysis with the discussion in the text. Which analysis did you find easier—this one or the analysis of your own life-cycle stage? Why?

3. Each population of age cohorts experiences similar historical influences as it moves through the life span. What are some of the influences experienced by your age cohorts? Discuss how these experiences have shaped your values, attitudes, and perception of the world.

4. Choose one life stage and one ethnic group, such as a Euro-American group, a Hispanic group, an Asian-American group, or a Native American group. For the life stage you have selected, analyze in detail the resources and obstacles the group you have chosen encounters at that life stage. After your analysis is complete, summarize your view of the ease with which members of that group are likely to perform the tasks of the life stage selected for study.

5. Bell (1976) identifies a double standard of aging in which men are described as getting "character lines" and their grey hair is seen as "distinguished," while women are described as becoming "old and wrinkled." Discuss this double standard in terms of the resources and obstacles supporting or inhibiting successful accomplishment of life-cycle tasks for men and women.

6. Discuss some of the resources and obstacles encountered by gay men and lesbians in old age. How do these differ from their heterosexual counterparts?

KEY TERMS

Double standard of aging Differential treatment of men and women as they progress through the late stages of the life cycle.

Historical cohort A group of people born at about the same time and who therefore experience similar historical events.

Life cycle   See Key Terms, Chapter 4.
Life-cycle stage   See Key Terms, Chapter 4.
Life tasks   See Key Terms, Chapter 4.
Reciprocity   As used in the context of this chapter, reciprocity refers to the mutuality and interdependence of roles.

As you have seen in this chapter, the life cycle encompasses a vast number of biological, psychological, social-structural, and cultural changes and adaptations. The two exhibits that follow illustrate some of them. The first looks at middle and late adulthood for men, examining some of the physical changes that occur and their psychological and social-structural effects. This exhibit is an interesting example of how life-cycle stages are experienced differently by members of different kinds of groups. The point is made that the physical changes of middle and late adulthood are related but different for men and women. Their impact is also different. For women, there is the need to adapt to the loss of child-bearing ability and all that is related to it. For men, the sense of masculine power and control is threatened. Both experiences are profoundly felt, yet they are tied to somewhat different social-structural arrangements. From a human-diversity perspective, one could then look at how these changes would be further differentiated for men and women from different ethnic groups, for lesbians and gay men, or for handicapped men and women.

The second exhibit, rather than starting with biological factors, begins with social-structural arrangements. The economic and political processes that have created and continue to maintain poverty for members of certain groups are shown to affect their biological and psychological functioning. The focus is on the elderly, but poverty is a similarly debilitating experience for any of its victims. The loss of hope, the despair, and the struggle to maintain one's physical and psychological health are commonly associated with poverty. Both of these exhibits, then, adopt a systems view. Each shows how any factor—biological, psychological, social-structural, or cultural—has important effects on each of the others.

5.1: MAN-O-PAUSE: THE CLIMACTERIC IN MEN

There's a story about two men, friends in their late 40s, who meet for lunch at a businessmen's restaurant.

"I've been kind of depressed lately," one confides. "I keep thinking about leaving home and sports cars and younger women. It must be male menopause."

"If that's male menopause," the friend replies, "I've had it since I was twelve."

Some controversy surrounds the "midlife crisis" in men. Endocrinologists, whose

continued

view of the climacteric in women tends to be confined to the hormonal changes of menopause itself, often take a dim view of the change of life in men. Although production of testosterone, the male sex hormone, decreases after age 40, hormonal changes occur more gradually in men than in women, with little or no physical discomfort.

Authorities who view the climacteric period in more cultural terms, however, believe that middle age is a time of significant personal change for most men, a time that, for lack of a better term, they call "male menopause."

Like the climacteric in women, the change of life in men involves subtle inter-actions among changes in men's bodies, how they view themselves, and how they are perceived by others.

Men's most visible—and most threatening—age-related physical change is balding. Although some men begin to lose their hair earlier in life, balding happens to most men during middle age. Balding is not only a mark of growing older, it's a major blow to some men's self-esteem. Concerns about hair loss are near the top of the list of questions about aging asked of the *Playboy* Advisor, and the enormous number of hair replacement products—hair implants, hair weaves, toupees, and "amazing lotions" that "cure baldness"—attest to the depth of men's feelings about losing their hair. In this context, the biblical story of Samson takes on new meaning: When he lost his hair, he lost everything.

Another physical dimension of aging in men concerns the prostate, the gland at the base of the back that produces most of men's seminal fluid. As men grow older, the prostate tends to grow larger, a condition called benign prostatic hypertrophy (BPH). BPH tends to pinch the urethra and causes decreased urine flow and a feeling of increased urinary urgency, especially at night. A diet rich in zinc has been shown to some extent to prevent BPH, and zinc supplements are sometimes recommended for this condition. Zinc-rich foods include: whole grains, milk, nuts, fresh peas and carrots, and oysters, reputed since ancient times to be a "virility food." BPH may also be treated surgically, through an operation called transurethral resection (TUR). An estimated 10% of men who have a TUR develop erection problems afterward.

The older a man grows, the greater his risk of developing prostate cancer, which accounts for 17% of cancers in men and 10% of men's cancer deaths. Prostate cancer is treated with either female sex hormones or prostatectomy, surgical removal of the gland. The hormone treatments tend to cause erection problems, and prostatectomy causes erection

continued

loss in about 90% of men. Some research suggests that a zinc-rich diet may prevent prostate cancer, but if you take zinc supplements in pill form, do not exceed the recommended dose because toxic reactions are possible.

Men should have their prostate glands checked by a physician annually, starting around age 35. This means getting an annual physical. Unlike women who get annual Pap tests and pelvic exams, most men rarely visit physicians during their 20s and 30s, and get out of the habit of thinking they'll ever need annual check-ups. It's a good idea to try to get back into annual physicals during the mid-30s, and certainly by age 40.

Men DO NOT automatically develop erection problems as they grow older. More stimulation may be necessary for erection and/or ejaculation, but men can enjoy marvelous lovemaking throughout their entire lives. Heart attack victims used to be told to refrain from lovemaking because it was believed to strain the heart. Now men with heart disease are encouraged to make love. Studies show that making love places less strain on the heart than merging into freeway traffic during rush hour. Some physicians recommend testosterone replacement therapy for older men who develop sex problems. Beware of this. Testosterone treatments have produced spotty,

uninspiring results (sex therapy works better), and they may stimulate the development of prostate cancer.

Depression is a common problem among women during the climacteric; the same is true to a lesser extent for men. Men's rates of suicide, divorce, and extramarital affairs increase in frequency from age 40 to 60. Men's careers also tend to peak and they must adjust to the fact that all their aspirations may not be fulfilled. During middle age, men long-socialized to control things must learn to give up some control: over their bodies, their careers, their children, and often their wives. They also confront their own mortality more painfully as they watch their friends die.

Men's reactions to growing older do not appear to be pre-ordained, but rather, are reflections of how American culture treats the aging process. Margaret Mead, the distinguished cultural anthro-pologist, has written that in cultures where the oldest members are the most revered, aging is neither traumatic nor depressing—it's welcomed.

Older men need the same things older women need: support, understanding, and information about aging in good health. Some basic changes in the general attitude toward aging wouldn't hurt either.

—SOURCE: Medical Self-Care,
Winter 1981, pp 16-17.

5.2: POVERTY

"We go into the supermarket and look at what other people eat all the time, and we can't afford it. The message we get is that we are not worthwhile. We are too darn old and useless, and no one really cares what happens to us."

Mr. Brown is 81 years old and his wife is 75. They live in a small house "way out in the woods" in central New Hampshire. Their isolated location makes it necessary for them to have a telephone and a car—expenses that they can't really afford. A year ago, the town re-evaluated property and the Browns' annual taxes went from $50 to $500. Their house is precious to them, so they borrowed money to meet the expense. They're still paying back the loan. They are also struggling to pay medical bills that their Medicare doesn't cover.

Together, the Browns receive $522 a month in Social Security and $14 a month in food stamps. Though Mr. Brown worked all his life—"364 out of 365 days a year, having only Christmas off"—he never managed to put much aside in savings. It seemed that whenever any savings built up, an emergency came along and wiped it all out. So now the Browns depend entirely on their monthly Social Security and food stamps. Trying to keep a house and broken-down car repaired, pay taxes, medical bills and other expenses doesn't leave them much for food. A typical day's meals are: cereal for breakfast, hamburg or potatoes for lunch, and a can of soup to share for dinner. The Browns drink water or tea with their meals. If they're careful, they can afford a pot roast once a month.

In spite of their need, the Browns are humilated to go to the welfare office and ask for help. "I feel like nobody when I walk in there," says Mr. Brown. "I have to tell them everything about myself and then I get fourteen dollars a month in stamps and threats on their Statement of Benefits that if I earn any money and don't report it to them immediately I can be dropped from food stamps. It makes me angry. I've worked hard all my life and I don't deserve this kind of treatment. We might as well not exist."

—SOURCE: Citizen's Commission on Hunger in New England. American Hunger Crisis: Poverty and Health in New England. Boston: Harvard University School of Public Health, 1984.

ADDITIONAL READINGS

Atchley, R. (1980). *The social forces of adult life.* Belmont, CA: Wadsworth Press.

Bernard, J. (1981). *The female world.* New York: The Free Press.

Bloom, M. (1980). *Life span human development.* New York: Macmillan.

Bloom, M. (1984). *Configurations of human behavior.* New York: Macmillan.

Bronfrenbrenner, U. (1979). *The ecology of human development.* Cambridge, MA: Harvard University Press.

Chunn, J. et al. (Eds.). (1983). *Mental health and people of color.* Washington, D.C.: Howard University Press.

Cox, H. (1984). *Later life: The realities of aging.* Englewood Cliffs, NJ: Prentice-Hall.

Erikson, E. (1964). *Childhood and society* (2nd ed.). New York: W.W. Norton.

Finkelhor, D. et al. (Eds.). (1983). *The dark side of families.* Beverly Hills, CA: Sage Publications.

Garbarino, J. (1982). *Children and families in the social environment.* Chicago: Aldine Publishing Co.

Kalish, R. (1973). *Late adulthood: Perspectives on human development.* Monterey, CA. Brooks-Cole Publishing Co.

Kubler-Ross, E. (1971). *Death: The final stage of growth.* Englewood Cliffs, NJ: Prentice-Hall.

Levinson, D. (1978). *The seasons of a man's life.* New York: Alfred A. Knopf.

Paul, W. et al. (Eds.). (1982). *Homosexuality: Social, psychological, and biological issues.* Beverly Hills, CA: Sage Publications.

Richmond-Abbott, M. (1983). *Masculine and feminine: Sex roles over the life cycle.* Reading, MA: Addison-Wesley Publishing Co.

Rogers, D. (1980). *Issues in life span development.* Monterey, CA: Brooks-Cole Publishing Co.

Steinberg, L. (Ed.). (1981). *The life cycle.* New York: Columbia University Press.

Troll, L. (1982). *Continuations: Adult development and aging.* Monterey, CA: Brooks-Cole Publishing Co.

Walsh, P. (1983). *Growing through time: An introduction to adult development.* Monterey, CA: Brooks-Cole Publishing Co.

Wilson, A. (1984). *Social services for older persons.* Waltham, MA: Little, Brown and Co.

REFERENCES

Bell, I. P. (1976). The double standard. In B.B. Hess (Ed.), *Growing old in America* (pp. 150-162). New Brunswick, NJ: Transaction Books.

Gilligan, C. (1982). *In a different voice: Psychological theory and human development.* Cambridge, MA: Harvard University Press.

Kimmel, D. (1980). *Adulthood and aging: An interdisciplinary developmental view* (2nd ed.). New York: Wiley.

Lowy, L. (1983). The older generation: What is due, what is owed? *Social Casework, 64*(6) 371-376.

Newman, B., & Newman, P. (1984). *Development through life: A psychosocial approach* (3rd ed.). Homewood, IL: Dorsey Press.

Rhodes, S. (1977). A developmental approach to the life cycle of the family. *Social Casework, 58*(5), 301-311.

Rosow, I. (1978). What is a cohort and why? *Human Development, 21*(3), 65-75.

6

USING KNOWLEDGE OF HUMAN BEHAVIOR IN PRACTICE

- CHAPTER OVERVIEW
- USING KNOWLEDGE TO COMMUNICATE EFFECTIVELY
- USING KNOWLEDGE TO RELATE EFFECTIVELY TO OTHERS
- USING KNOWLEDGE TO ASSESS PRACTICE SITUATIONS HOLISTICALLY
- USING KNOWLEDGE TO PLAN WITH OTHERS
- USING KNOWLEDGE TO CARRY OUT PLANS
- USING KNOWLEDGE FOR EVALUATION
- SUMMARY
- STUDY QUESTIONS
- KEY TERMS
- EXHIBIT 6.1: THE MANY DIMENSIONS OF CANCER CARE
- EXHIBIT 6.2: MEETING THE NEEDS OF CHILD ABUSE VICTIMS
- REFERENCES

CHAPTER OVERVIEW

This chapter is structured around the six elements of the problem-solving process first introduced in Chapter 1. These are communicating effectively with others, relating effectively to others, assessing situations holistically, planning with others, carrying out plans, and evaluating the outcomes of practice efforts. In this chapter, it will be shown how knowledge of human behavior is useful for carrying out problem-solving activities effectively. This reinforces the linkage between knowledge and practice discussed in the Preface. The emphasis is on knowledge, but practice is addressed much more explicitly than elsewhere in the book. At the end of this chapter you should be able to put your knowledge of human behavior to work in actual practice situations. You will be ready to draw from knowledge as the foundation for your practice activities, using it to make informed decisions at each stage of the problem-solving process. It is knowledge, a commitment to helping others, and the use of professional ethics that make effective professional helping possible.

USING KNOWLEDGE TO COMMUNICATE EFFECTIVELY

It will be helpful to begin by reviewing what is involved in **communication.** It is best described as a complex interactive process that includes the following elements (Day, 1977; McQuail, 1975):

1. **Encoding.** Putting a message into some form that enables it to be transmitted to others; forms of communication include verbal, written, and non-verbal ("body language") communication
2. **Sending.** Actually transmitting the message
3. **Static.** Factors that impede the transmission of messages
4. **Decoding.** Interpreting the message, which involves an accurate understanding of the form of the message.
5. **Response.** After receiving a message, initiating further communication by encoding a message in response to the one just received
6. **Sender.** The person who is encoding the message
7. **Receiver.** The person who is decoding the message

Communication is complex because messages are being sent in many forms, often quickly and in great volume. Also, persons who are communicating are both senders and receivers, because when receivers interpret a message and then respond, they become senders.

Developing communication skills requires an understanding of oneself, the people with whom one is communicating, and the context in which the communication occurs. Everyone filters messages because they encode and decode through their own value system and their own perception of the world in which they live. Focusing on values for a moment, it should be clear that they have an interesting effect on communication. For one thing, values tell us who we ought to communicate with. We seek to become close to people we love, respected by those we esteem, and accepted by those on whom we depend for employment or resources. People we define as unimportant are likely to be placed outside the arena in which we intend to communicate. For example, we may pay attention to our supervisor in an agency in which we work but pass by secretarial staff with hardly a look.

An interesting aspect of communication is that we are doing it all the time, even though we may be unaware of it. If we pass by secretaries without a look because we define them as unimportant parts of our agency environment, we are still communicating something to them. We may not intend to, nor even be aware that we are communicating, but we are. The act of walking past someone and not acknowledging them is a type of body language. It conveys the message we do not consider them important, even though we might not be intending to make this message public. The power of this kind of behavior is that its social acceptability makes individuals perpetuate it without conscious thought. This example makes clear, then, that we have to have a great deal of self-awareness in order to understand how others will be perceiving our communication through our intended and unintended behavior.

Of course, decoding is as important as encoding. We might walk by a secretary without any sort of acknowledgement because we are so preoccupied with some element of a case that we are unaware of our surroundings in general. The secretary, however, may decode our message quite differently. If we usually greet him/her in some way, feelings may be hurt. If we routinely ignore the secretary, s/he may interpret our passage as another statement of disdain. On the other hand, if we have a perplexed look on our face, the secretary may assume that we are preoccupied rather than disinterested. The same issues can arise with users of our services. They may interpret our distracted look as disinterest rather than seeing it as evidence that we are still mulling over a point made earlier in the discussion.

Language is similarly open to interpretation by the receiver. People who speak different languages may find communication very difficult. People who are not native speakers of a language may not understand subtle nuances and colloquial expressions used by native speakers. Even speakers of the same language may use dialects that make communication difficult. Two examples of this are very common. Black Americans have developed sub-cultural adaptations to English which reflect their need to survive in a social world that has often been hostile and restrictive (Morgan, 1980). Professional people have developed terminology that is difficult for outsiders to understand, again reflecting the specialized environments in which they work. Consider psychiatric terminology, medical terms, the use of abbreviations to refer to forms or procedures, and so on. The result is that even when people speak they do not necessarily communicate clearly. This becomes even more of a problem when there are "dialects" of body language as well, such as when a Native American refuses to look a professional person in the eye. The Native American is showing respect, but the professional may interpret such behavior as meaning that the other person is lying or is not very interested.

Even written communication is not necessarily interpreted accurately. Illiterate people have difficulty communicating in this way. People who are not used to bureaucratic procedures may find the receipt of form letters difficult to understand, and may interpret their impersonality as meaning that the letters are not very important. Memos and letters can be misplaced, creating serious blockages to communication. Testimony may be written in such a technical way that it is difficult to understand. Making people fill out forms and applications can produce very inaccurate communication. When people do not understand the reasons for them, or if they cannot understand the directions for completing them, forms may provide very inaccurate information and therefore impede accurate communication.

The ability to communicate effectively with others involves mastery of a lot of knowledge. Understanding ourselves is basic. How do we ourselves communicate, and how is our communication received by others? Why do we communicate as we do, and can we alter our communication patterns? This type of understanding goes back to biological, psychological, social-structural, and cultural factors. Do we have biological limits that make us slur our speech? Do we get so anxious in certain situations that we tend to stutter? The language(s) we speak reflect our cultural and social-structural characteristics, as do the values we hold. Similarly, our body language reflects many aspects of ourselves. A crippled arm that makes it impossible to shake hands will alter the way in which we approach and greet people. Lack of attention to our appearance may indicate to others that we are disorganized or psychologically depressed. Whether we greet people with a hug or with no physical contact can reflect our cultural and social-structural backgrounds.

These same variables are also important as we interpret the communication of others. We need to find out whether the chronic squinting of a user of services reflects poor vision (biological) or a sense of inadequacy (psychological). When offered coffee during a home visit, we need to know whether declining to have some will be interpreted as a violation of cultural or personal values. (If so, not accepting the coffee could impede further communication.) And when we visit a user in a home environment that appears messy or dilapidated, we have to make a realistic assessment of the social-structural realities of that person's life rather than immediately imposing our own standards of good houskeeping. As we interact with users in situations that may differ from what we are used to, we have to be careful that our own body language is not sending messages of disapproval and discomfort. Obviously, our understanding of, and respect for human diversity is a critical element in our ability to communicate accurately and effectively.

There is another way in which understanding the environment in which communication occurs is very important. Static, as you will recall, is anything that interferes with the transmission process. Many of the things already discussed—value differences, language differences, and so on—can produce static. However, the physical environment itself may also be significant. Communicating by telephone limits body language to tone of voice. Speaking in a noisy room may increase opportunities for words to be misunderstood or not heard. Communicating in an agency environment in which the user feels very uncomfortable may inhibit and distort the communication that occurs. Communicating through letters or electronic media such as television or audiotapes, limits opportunities for clarification and interaction. This in turn increases the potential for barriers to full communication.

Communicating effectively with others, then, is a good example of how professional helpers must strive to understand the person in the environment. The biological, psychological, social-structural, and cultural characteristics of people strongly affect how, what, and when they communicate. Communication is also influenced by the environment in which it occurs. As importantly, the helping person affects the communication process through his/her own participation. In order to communicate effectively as a professional helper, you will have to skillfully apply all of the knowledge of human behavior that has been discussed in previous chapters.

USING KNOWLEDGE TO RELATE EFFECTIVELY TO OTHERS

A professional **helping relationship** involves establishing a base for working together to solve problems (Gilbert, Miller & Specht, 1980). Trust is fundamental. It enables people to share the information and feelings that make it possible to discuss, analyze, and meet needs. Trust involves many things, including: the belief that information will be kept confidential (Wilson, 1978); that the people involved are genuinely interested in each other; that real feelings and beliefs can be expressed without fear of punishment or humiliation; that there is a reasonable degree of reciprocity and equality in the relationship: that the professional helping person is competent.

Knowledge of psychological variables is relevant to understanding how relationships can be built and maintained. People who are unusually suspicious may have difficulty trusting others. Those who have a weak self-image may be reluctant to share information because they don't consider anything about themselves to be very important. Reluctance to share information may also be an issue with people who are very proud and for whom achievement is very important. Anything that they feel reflects badly on them is likely to be avoided or hidden. Manipulative people often try to control interaction, making it difficult to relate openly and with some degree of equality. The helping person must be able to recognize these and other aspects of psychological behavior in order to decide how to most effectively build a professional relationship.

Social-structural variables are similarly important. Status differentials between people often impede relationships. A helping person may find a wealthy executive, who is also a user of services, difficult to work with because s/he finds it awkward and painful to be in what s/he considers a dependent position. Abused children may believe that helping people will use their power in the same way as their parents, and therefore be equally frightened of them. People in the criminal justice system may fear that any information that is shared will be used against them. The nature of social structures is that people interact with others in prescribed ways—some have more status, power, or resources than others. This can make it difficult to develop an interpersonal environment in which people feel that they can be honest and still be accepted in spite of their situation. Unless these social-structural variables are understood, establishing an effective helping relationship may prove an elusive goal.

Naturally, cultural factors are also important. People may have beliefs and values that define the whole helping process as unacceptable, and therefore be very reluctant to become involved (Landy, 1965). Other values may relate to the environment in which helping occurs, or who provides it. Helping may be seen as something that ought to occur at home or in church, rather than in a social agency. Members of one's own group may be seen as the only acceptable helpers in other instances (Good Tracks, 1973). Values about dealing with women or members of other minority groups can be additional issues in some cases. The helping person's values can also be significant, as when there are strongly held beliefs about birth control, abortion, child abuse, and other behaviors. In all these instances, cultural and subcultural beliefs may serve to make it more difficult to establish a meaningful professional relationship. Addressing these issues depends on the ability of the helper to understand them. Developing an effective helping relationship takes sensitivity, skill, and knowledge. It is clear that there are a number of psychological, social-structural, and cultural issues that can impede relationship formation. Being able to sort out what issue is blocking efforts to form a particular helping relationship is basic to finding solutions that will work.

USING KNOWLEDGE TO ASSESS PRACTICE SITUATIONS HOLISTICALLY

The success of helping efforts depends on how well the problematic situation is understood and how many resources are identified to help address that situation. This is, as we saw earlier, the process of assessment. The generalist professional helping person seeks to address all aspects of the problematic situation. As each dimension is identified and understood, appropriate resources are sought. As was pointed out in Chapter 1, this can include the involvement of specialized helping persons (surgeons, police officers, remedial reading specialists, and so on) who address specific aspects of the problematic situation. The generalist maintains a holistic view by managing the total package of resources.

In specific practice situations, one or more of the four major categories of behavior (biological, psychological, social-structural, and cultural) may not be problematic. For example, a situation of child abuse might or might not include biological elements. In one case, the abusive parent may have a brain tumor creating headaches. The noise and movement that the child generates might increase the pain and lead the parent to beat the child. In this example, there is a biological element (the brain tumor) affecting the parent's abusive behavior as well as the type of abuse the child receives (a beating). A different abusive parent may be well physically, but may face economic pressures (social-structural) that lead to non-physical child abuse. In this case the abuse might take the form of verbal threats and curses that undermine the child's sense of security and well-being (psychological abuse). In this second example, no specific biological elements are involved in the abusive situation. We can see, then, that assessing practice situations requires that the biological, psychological, social-structural, and cultural aspects of behavior be systematically explored. Some may be judged not to be especially relevant for a given practice situation, but each must be checked as a possible element.

These aspects of behavior are checked not just as part of the problem. Each may also offer resources that could be helpful in addressing the situation. Continuing the child-abuse example, let us say that the abuse has been primarily psychological, with the child having internalized a negative self-image and having developed a fearful relationship with the abusing parent. As a result, the child may also eat poorly and be small and underweight for its age. Peers might then make fun of the child and thereby serve to reinforce its sense of isolation and inadequacy. In this instance, a goal of the helping effort might be to improve the eating patterns of the child and involve it in exercise programs that facilitate growth. This will hopefully improve the child's peer-support network. This, in turn, can strengthen the child's ability to tolerate the lack of psychological support at home until that situation is changed. We can see, then, how biological growth could be a resource in a situation that involves primarily psychological and/or social-structural problems.

If situations are incompletely assessed, it is unlikely that the helping plans that are developed will be sufficient. Generally, helping professionals will build plans around the problem as they understand it. If they do not see some aspect of behavior as problematic, they are not likely to try to find a solution. This, of course, can lead to incomplete and ineffective problem-solving efforts. Because human behavior is so systemic, omitting one part of a system will have internal effects as well as affecting other systems. Even though many things may be assessed accurately, and effective helping plans developed, the things that are overlooked may keep interfering. As a result, problems continue in spite of helping efforts. This can be discouraging for helper and user alike.

The child-abuse example we have been using can further illustrate this point. If the parent does indeed have a brain tumor which is the source of the abusive behavior toward the child, the tumor has to be treated before the parent's behavior is likely to change. However, the helper may instead focus on the behavior itself and decide that psychological factors are causing it. Assume the parent is a widower who has had difficulty handling his grief. The helper sees the abusive behavior toward the child as resulting from grief, a sense of loss, and feelings of abandonment, rather than from a biological illness. Counseling may be provided as a result and, while it may be helpful in resolving remaining issues around the loss of the spouse, it may not have much effect on the child-abuse situation. Eventually, of course, the helper's on-going evaluation of helping efforts (to be discussed in more detail later in this chapter) will probably lead him/her to reassess the causes of the headaches and the resulting abusive behavior. In the meantime, however, the problematic situation continues.

It is common for helping professionals to tend to emphasize one aspect of behavior over others. Specialists, of course, would be expected to do this. Even generalists, though, can sometimes have biases toward certain sources of behavior. Most often this bias is toward psychological factors that affect people's actions. The kind of holistic perspective on human behavior developed in this book should help to avoid limiting one's view of practice situations. Unless assessment is holistic, it is not likely to be completely accurate. Those aspects of behavior that are overlooked then have the potential for exerting influences that are neither recognized nor addressed. When this happens, helping is less effective than it otherwise could be.

USING KNOWLEDGE TO PLAN WITH OTHERS

Planning is a function of both helpers and users. People seeking help have the ultimate responsibility for their own lives. It is not the responsibility or right of professional helpers to decide what other people ought to do. They can only help them to think through options and strategies for attaining their goals. The user, then, must participate actively in deciding what will be done. The helping person provides information, emotional support, and guidance, so that decisions are made in an orderly way. But the helping person does not control the planning process.

Planning grows directly out of assessment. **Planning** is the process whereby specific activities are identified by helpers and users which they believe will help resolve the problematic situation. These activities may involve many people, not only helpers and users of services. Pincus and Minahan, for example, talk about target and action systems. The target system is "people who need to be changed to accomplish the goals of the change agent," while the action system is "the change agent and the people he works with and through to accomplish his goals and influence the target system" (Pincus & Minahan, 1973, p. 63). In this terminology, the change agent refers to the professional helper and, of course "he" and "his" should more accurately be read as "s/he" and "his/her." The point is that often many people are involved in helping activities. A corporation may be the user, seeking help to reduce alcoholism and absenteeism among workers. Working with a social worker, the company may involve its executive staff, union personnel, insurance companies that provide health benefits for its workers, a range of social agencies in the community, and, of course, its work force. In this instance, planning would have to take into account all of these groups, many of which might also be involved in the planning process. Involving as many relevant people as possible in the planning process is important, because when people are involved they are more likely to take responsibility for what happens.

Planning requires a great amount of knowledge. The planning process itself involves knowledge about psychological and group functioning. How can people's resistance to, or fear of planning be overcome? In many instances, self-help groups can be developed or used to provide support and additional information for people as they plan for change. Cultural differences may also be relevant. In some cases, whole extended-family networks may have to be involved in planning for individual family members. This reflects cultural values of respect for family activity. And, of course, social-structural variables can be very significant. Workers who want better protection from hazardous working conditions cannot achieve this goal by themselves. The company for which they work will have to be involved in some way.

But planning also involves other kinds of information. The helping professional must know what resources are available, how to connect with them, and how they can best be used (Sauber, 1983). In many communities, directories of services are available to help with this task. Knowing about resources goes beyond simply knowing what exists, however. The professional helper must also know which among the available options is likely to be the best choice in particular situations. For example, assessment may indicate the need for psychotherapy. As planning proceeds, the decision has to be made about what kind to seek: individual or group? traditional or cognitive-behavioral? And which kind of traditional therapy, if that is selected: Freudian, Jungian, or Adlerian? (Brody, 1981). Another example is when assessment indicates that diet should be modified. Decisions are needed about how to do this. It could occur by being hospitalized for a period, or simply being under a doctor's care. It can also be accomplished by people supplementing their eating patterns with pills that can be obtained over the counter. Each strategy will affect diet, but the mechanisms will differ considerably (Brody, 1979). Whatever the problematic situation, knowing what resources are available, how they can be used effectively, and how people can be involved so that they will actively participate involves knowledge of the biological, psychological, social-structural, and cultural dimensions of human behavior.

USING KNOWLEDGE TO CARRY OUT PLANS

Planning, as we have seen, involves deciding what will be done and who will do it. Activities will generally be carried out by the helping professional, the user of services, and a variety of others who are involved in the various aspects of the problematic situation. The helping person may serve as a resource for all of these people, assisting them to accomplish their particular tasks. In order to do this, helpers should have sufficient knowledge to provide information effectively to others, teach people skills and share information with them, and provide emotional support.

Knowledge is needed to carry out a range of other interventive skills, as well (Zastrow, 1981). The skills of generalist professional helpers are almost endless, it seems. They link people with needed resources; advocate for the needs of people who are ignored or discriminated against; provide counseling and/or therapy; mobilize people to act on their own behalf; help people modify behavior that they have decided they wish to change; participate in policy making; participate in research efforts to better understand human behavior; and write documents of many kinds to share information with others. Each of these skills is grounded in a body of knowledge. Mastering all of these skills, therefore, entails a command of a wide-ranging knowledge base that includes the biological, psychological, social-structural, and cultural dimensions of human behavior.

To reinforce the link between knowledge and the skills enumerated above, think back to our earlier discussion of communication. We saw that understanding communication and being able to use specific communication techniques in a purposeful way grew out of knowledge of the communication process. The same is true for any of the skills that professional helpers use in their practice. The knowledge needed includes that which underlies the skill itself, as well as knowledge of human behavior that directs choices about when and how to use the skill. For example, consider linking people with resources. First, the helper must know how to locate resources by using a directory, talking with colleagues, or utilizing some other source of information. Then the helper must be able to understand what various resources are likely to do (remember our discussion of the many types of psychotherapy, necessitating a decision about which one is appropriate for a particular user). Knowledge of the procedures through which linkage will occur is also important. Many times applications have to be processed or interviews are required, for example. Finally knowledge of users and their situation is important. Some people can accept information and use it. Others are more resistant, or do not know how to translate information into concrete behavior. Still others need considerable help and support in carrying out the mechanics of making contact with a resource.

Carrying out plans, then, requires skills of many kinds. Each, in turn, requires knowledge. Without constant reference to the knowledge base of skill activity, skills tend to become mechanical. They are applied without a clear sense of how they could be used most effectively. This makes it easier to fall into strategies for carrying out plans that are comfortable for the helping person, but which may not be especially helpful for users of services. While plans tell helpers what to do, the way they carry out these plans through their specific activities depends on their commitment and their knowledge about how to use helping skills most effectively.

USING KNOWLEDGE FOR EVALUATION

The purpose of professional helping is to help people function more effectively so as to better attain their life goals. As helping efforts proceed, they must be monitored to make sure that they are achieving the goals for which they were selected. If they are not, there is no point in continuing. New plans are needed that will be more effective, or existing plans need to be rethought so that more effective strategies for implementing them are selected.

The evaluation of helping outcomes requires a somewhat different body of knowledge than we have discussed in this book. There is a body of information about collecting and analyzing data that is relevant to the evaluation of social welfare programs (Babbie, 1979; Williams & Elmore, 1976). This knowledge comes from the social sciences and is an application of the scientific method to the evaluation of social programs. There is also a strong link with social policy, because programs are usually evaluated in terms of the purposes for which they were created (Rogers, Doron & Jones, 1979). However, the effectiveness of practice activities should also be assessed in relation to the purposes of the practice effort. The planning stage, discussed earlier, establishes purposes for helping efforts. However, definitions of how one will know whether these purposes have been achieved reflect cultural and social-structural factors. An agency (social-structural) may define the number of contacts with users of services as the criterion for defining successful helping. The users themselves may be more interested in the quality of the interaction during each contact, the degree to which they were able to make decisions for themselves, or the way in which they were treated during the helping effort. Our knowledge of culture and social structures helps us understand why formal organizations like bureaucracies may have different criteria for success than do the various cultural groups whom they serve. Cultural values pertaining to equality and justice are also relevant in evaluating outcomes. An agency may simply aggregate data about services and find that they indicate generally satisfactory outcomes. Hidden in these data, however, may be the fact that most of those for whom outcomes were not satisfactory were members of minority groups.

Another way in which knowledge of human behavior helps to evaluate outcomes is by maintaining a holistic perspective. Many people complain that the care they get in hospitals is unsatisfactory, yet hospitals are able to document that their care is successful in treating illness. What is happening, of course, is that people place treatment within the context of their whole life experience. Having to wait for service, having difficulty paying for increasingly expensive medical care, being isolated from family members, and being treated by many different specialists who never relate to each other are all common complaints of people who have been ill. People want to feel in control of what is happening to them. The hospital, on the other hand, is primarily concerned with each specific helping act rather than the whole person. Were injections given when needed? Was the bed linen changed? Were operations performed on schedule and competently?

Both perspectives are relevant in evaluating outcomes. Yet it is possible for the outcome to be deemed successful from one point of view, and not successful from the other. Therefore, one of the functions of the generalist professional helping person is to try to mediate between organizations and the people they serve. Organizations can be helped to be more responsive to the total person, and people can learn how to use specialized services more effectively so that all their needs are met (Spingarn, 1982). Evaluating outcomes from the point of view of the provider of services as well as the user makes it more likely that this will occur (MacNair, Wodarski & Giordano, 1982).

SUMMARY

The purpose of this chapter has been to lead you beyond knowing for its own sake so that you can begin to *use* your knowledge to do things. Professional helping people are oriented toward action—helping others. At each stage in the problem-solving process, knowledge provides a critical base from which decisions are made and activities undertaken. The exhibits that end the chapter provide two very different examples of how important knowledge is for providing effective help. The knowledge of human behavior that you have been reviewing and expanding throughout this book has, here at the end of this chapter, become a highly significant part of your practice competence. We can now go back to the very beginning of the book to reinforce a point made at that time: A commitment to helping others is fundamental for effective helping. However, it must be linked with the knowledge that makes the professional helper far more than just a well-meaning and caring person. Professional helping grows out of the twin roots of commitment and knowledge. From these roots emerge the skillful activities through which problematic situations are analyzed and resolved.

STUDY QUESTIONS

1. Think about something that is problematic for you now (it might even be the course for which you are reading this book!). Assess this situation by first identifying its biological, psychological, social-structural, and cultural dimensions. Remember that not all of these may be involved, but be sure to think through each carefully before deciding whether or not it is relevant. Then use the same categories to lay out the resources that are (or might be) available to you for solving the problem.

2. Continuing with the situation in the previous question, now engage in the planning process. What courses of action are open to you for solving the problem given the resources that you have identified? (Remember that resources can also be obstacles, so the use of some resources might create other problems.) Identify the people who would also have to be involved were you to adopt various strategies for addressing your problem.

3. The problem-solving process as used in professional helping bears a close relationship to the scientific method. On a sheet of paper, list the six parts of the problem-solving process down the left side. Then list the parts of the scientific method down the right side. At the bottom summarize the similarities and differences that you see.

4. This chapter has emphasized the link between knowledge and effective practice. Do you see any problems in this relationship? For example, do you think that it takes so long to think about everything that action might be too slow? Or that no one can possibly know all that they should? What other issues occur to you? Can you think of any strategies for dealing with the issues that you have identified?

5. Now that you have completed this book, take a moment to reflect. On a sheet of paper, list the five most important things, in your opinion, that you have learned. Then list three to five things that you would now like to learn. Finally, list specific actions you could take to learn the things that you have identified.

KEY TERMS

Communication Interaction between people which involves the transmission of information between senders and receivers through the use of encoding and decoding. Communication occurs verbally, through body language, and in writing.

Evaluation Using specific data to decide whether the outcomes identified in the planning process were actually achieved.

Helping relationship Establishing a base for working together to solve problems.

Planning The process whereby specific activities are identified by helpers and users that they believe will help resolve problematic situations.

To end this book, two very different human problems are presented. They illustrate the range of knowledge needed to solve human problems effectively. Exhibit 6.1 demonstrates the effective use of knowledge to cure a young man's cancer. Even in this case, however, some aspects of the young man's life—such as his need to be loved and to love—were only partially understood and addressed. Exhibit 6.2 is not as encouraging. It explores the complexities of child abuse, and shows how complete knowledge of abusive situations is often lacking. As a result, many helping efforts fail—and many children die. As you read these two exhibits, try to put yourself in the position of a professional helping person with responsibility for these people. What would you need to know to communicate effectively with a black teenager who has cancer? Or how could you use your knowledge of biological, psychological, social-structural, and cultural factors to develop a professional relationship with an abusing parent or an abused child? What are the critical areas of behavior to assess when child abuse is suspected? And, who needs to be involved in planning to stop abuse? (remember Pincus and Minahan's concept of target and action systems). Here, at the end of the book, you should be ready to appreciate the meanings of these questions. We also hope you realize that you have much knowledge that enables you to answer them and, in so doing, to recognize your growing competence as a professional helper.

6.1 THE MANY DIMENSIONS OF CANCER CARE

I loved running. It was my whole life. I'd go to school, go to work, but track was everything. I was only 18, and the coach was encouraging me. So when they told me I might never run again, man, I just didn't want to live anymore.

He's 25, has a handsome, sensitive face, close-cropped hair, the soft, trusting eyes of a child and the lean body of a runner.

We were in his bedroom in the Brown family apartment in Brooklyn, a room decorated with bright posters: a leopard, a dragon, a blue pirate ship and a Jolly Green Giant.

First, I had this bike accident in June when I hit a car. It bruised my knee and sent me spinning up into the air, but somehow I came down on my feet next to the curb. I guess the trauma and everything on my

continued

knee was the beginning of it— how the cancer started to move.

A couple of weeks later, I went roller-skating and banged my knee against an iron pole, in the same spot. The pain was so terrific I had to go home.

I laid off it for a week, and the pain went away. So I went to practicing track. The pain stayed away for two weeks, and I went roller-skating again, but my friend, by accident, kicked me in the same spot. This time the pain was so real I almost passed out.

The pain didn't leave me, so I told my mother to take me to Brooklyn Jewish Hospital. I didn't want to go; I was scared of hospitals, except at Brooklyn Jewish I had friends since I was working there as a TV attendant, putting sets in rooms for the patients.

They gave me a whole series of tests and exercises and finally saw like a spot in my knee above the tibia area. The bone doctor came over and said they would have to do a biopsy. Right then, I started to shake and get scared.

I had a biopsy done, and the results were . . . . *(Pauses, unable to say it.)* I couldn't bear the results, man. When he told me there was a malignant tumor, I couldn't believe I had cancer.

My doctor knew I was taking it hard, and he told me he was going to get me the best care, so I would have to go to Memorial Hospital. I asked him, "You think they can fix me so I can run again?"

He sent me to the big bone man at Memorial, Dr. Joseph Lane. When I got there, I had butterflies, and I was scared. Then I met Dr. Lane, and he lifted my spirits; he was beautiful to me. From the way he came across to me, it gave me so much faith that I said, "I can handle whatever it takes."

So I got settled into the hospital, and that week I went through a whole series of tests. When it was over, Dr. Lane came in and said I had osteogenic sarcoma—cancer of the bone. I asked if maybe I could have a bone replacement so I wouldn't lose my leg, and he said he'd do what was possible. But first I had to do a chemotherapy treatment to shrink the size of the tumor. When it was over, he would see what was possible for me.

Anita, the nurse who gave me the chemo, set me up for the first treatment, and I was worried about my hair. I said, "Once that goes, man, I don't know. I'm gonna lose something inside." It took about four days. When I saw my hair falling out, man, I just about passed out. I was telling my sister, "Braid my hair for the last time." She braided it up good, and then everything just fell out, and I said, "Oh no!"

This was just the beginning. It shocked me, and my mind was really confused because there was going to be 22 of these treatments. So Anita had a patient, Jimmy, I think his name was, come to talk to me. He had

continued

been going there for two years and was on his last treatment. He told me, "James, in the beginning, it's real tough. Martin Luther King said he climbed to the mountaintops, and it's like that—climbing to the mountaintops—when you're fighter cancer. You're gonna have your ups and downs and your moments when you call it quits." Then he said, "You gotta stick it out, because there's only one ball game here, and it's your own life. You got no choice. You got to play to win if you want to stay on this earth." Talking that way, he really got deep into me, he scared me. But then I said, "I can handle this; I can take these treatments without a hassle."

Every Tuesday morning. I went to get treatments. I was so weak when I left the hospital, I'd be throwing up sometimes coming through the front door. When I got home, I shut myself off from the family and every-thing. I'd turn to this room and close the door. I had a lot of complications from the medicine. It got so I couldn't take any more.

I was on my eighth treatment, and Anita said, "It's time for your surgery, we'll finish the rest of the treatments later." It was the first week in December. There was this other girl, a nurse helper, I met at the hospital. She's Patricia Brown, just 20 years old, and we used to call each other Mr. and Mrs. Brown. I got very fond of this girl.

On the night before surgery, Dr. Lane came into my room to tell me the results of the final tests. I was still hoping to have a bone replacement, not an amputation, but he said the tests showed the tumor was all around a main nerve in the leg. If they had to sever that while taking out the tumor, my leg would be paralyzed, and I'd be dragging it around for the rest of my life. Right there, everything I hoped for, the whole idea of a bone replacement, was dwindling away.

The way Dr. Lane was explaining it, my best option was the amputation. I asked, "Where would you do it?" He showed me here *(points to midthigh)* and my heart was breaking because I never thought it'd be so high up.

I thought about the possibilities, and I told him I wanted the amputation. Dr. Lane stayed with me in my room for about an hour, talking to me, keeping my spirits up. If it hadn't been for him, I would never have made it that night. Dr. Lane is the most beautiful person I've ever met.

My life was different before I experienced all this. I had never met so many wonderful people before. They give you so much confidence.

A male nurse came to my room. He said. "I'm here to shave

continued

your leg." I said, "O.K., man, come on and do the job." So we started talking. He was a young guy like me, and he said, "How did all this occur?" I told him I used to run track and was heavy into it. He said, "For this to happen to you makes me very sad." He'd been shaving my leg, just breezing along, but then he started shaving it real slow, taking extra care like he didn't want to hurt it no more, giving it all respect like it was going to stay with me. I was feeling him caring so much for me. It's having the caring and loving around you that helps you make it.

In the morning, the nurse came by to give me the injection to make me drowsy. I'm looking down the hall, waiting for the guy with the strecher to come along. My ma, my sister, my grand-mother, my cousins from Queens were all there.

Finally the attendant came to get me. I had this feeling that I won't be seeing my leg no more, and I was talking to my leg. I said, "Well, old buddy, it's going to be kind of hard to get over the loss of you. You've brought me my desire, my hopes, my dreams, but things happen for a purpose—it's a thing we have to accept."

When I woke up, I was in the recovery room with some nurse bending over me. Then I woke up again in my room, and who was standing there but Patricia. She's from Trinidad and has the most beautiful smile and face. She gave me a kiss and then I looked down and didn't see my leg, just the flat bed cover, and I said, "Well, I guess they did it."

I was falling asleep, but Patricia was kissing me again, and I felt wet from her tears. That woke me up real fast, and I said, "What's the matter?" "Nothing," she said, "I never loved anybody like this before."

After a few weeks, Dr. Lane sent me home from the hospital, so for a while I had to go to the Rusk Institute for the final fitting of the prosthesis and to learn how to walk up ramps and other obstacles. I was still getting around on my crutches, so my girlfriend, Patricia, would come by every morning to take me into town on her way to school.

She'd left Memorial to go to a Catholic college in Yonkers, and me and her were very close. But I was also getting this complex about my missing leg, wondering what she was going to think when I got the prosthesis, how we'd be able to make it, like when she wanted to go dancing or to the beach.

One day, we're in the car, and we have this talk. I said, "How come you like a man with no leg?" She says, "Because I love the man. The legs don't matter." Then I said what was bothering me. "How do I know

continued

you're not just staying with me because you think I'm a charity case?"

She looked at me real sad and said, "How could you say that?" She began to cry and said, "Everything was going so good. Why did you come out and say such a hurting episode?"

I apologized and said I was all mixed up, but after that it was never the same again. Then one day she enlisted in the Air Force and went off to Kansas. I really loved that girl and I just drove her away.

When I got the new leg, I started walking straight like everyone else, and I also started to get straightened out in the head. I was doing the last part of my chemotherapy, and I just walked in there, man, with my new prosthesis. Anita and my friends on the 17th floor were cheering and applauding like this was some kind of hero. Right there, I felt better, and then Anita, she had me as a spokesman for some new patients with problems.

One of them was this 9-year-old boy who was giving his mother a hard time about taking the pills. He was stubborn, man, really stubborn. So I pressured him. I was trying my damnedest, and I wondered, "Where does a 9-year-old get all this strength to say no?" I thought about how desperate I was once and how much terror must be inside his

little heart, and I pleaded with him. But nothing worked.

A couple of treatments later, he started to get the hang of it, and we became friends. His name was Eddie. I asked him, "You ride skateboards?" He said, "Yeah." So I told him, "There might be a possibility you will lose your leg." He looked at me kind of sad, but then I demonstrated how I walked with my prosthesis, and I told him how I could ride bikes again. I wanted him to know that if he lost his leg, he could function normally.

The next thing you know, he is hugging me like I was his big brother, saying if me and him hang out together like I promised, he was going to surprise everybody and get well real fast. Then he said, "When I get well, if you need something, I'll go on my bike and get it for you." *(Breaks up, unable to continue.)* This is very touching to me.

You see, he was believing me, and right there me and him was like one person almost, so close. I was going along without my girl, with nobody real close. Then, before I know what's happening, this little boy is with me. It's like you can't go very far all alone by yourself.

I never used to pay no mind to handicaps or anything. But now, I'm one of those people, a statistic. Only there's millions of us out there, walking without legs, making it without arms. I just feel

continued

for those people because, like we got parts of us that's missing, but what's left is more one piece, more concentrated in caring and loving. So we're like everyone else, you know, only more so because of this.

—SOURCE: Curtis Bill Pepper, "The Victors." The New York Times Magazine, January 29, 1984, pp. 14ff.

6.2: MEETING THE NEEDS OF CHILD ABUSE VICTIMS

It always came down to a single question: Should an abused child be taken away from its parents?

City social workers, handling up to 30 cases of reported child abuse each month, will respond to an anticipated 35,000 reports of child abuse—a record number—in New York City's five boroughs this year. Overworked and awash in paper work, they are legally mandated both to protect children's live's and to try to keep families together.

"It's the most difficult job in the world to work with children being abused or neglected by their parents," said Bernard M. Shiffman, the executive director of the Community Coucil of Greater New York, a major voluntary welfare organization. "Society and the court system say the family is sacred. But some families shouldn't be families. To be in the middle of that, you have to be Solomon."

A report last week by Priscilla Hall, the Inspector General of New York City's Human Resources Administration, the city's umbrella welfare agency, found serious failures in the city's handling of such cases.

After repeated complaints by a city social worker, the Inspector General found that city welfare officials were seriously negligent in the handling of 17 abuse cases in which 9 Brooklyn children died. Gail M. Kong, the director of the city's Office of Special Services for Children, said the cases were only a small portion of the 9,000 reports of child abuse that the Brooklyn welfare office receives yearly, but she conceded that problems had been uncovered that needed attention.

What follow are cases drawn from the report's detailed histories of abused children. They illustrate the hard choices—and sometimes the wrong choices—made by social workers dealing with broken homes, teen-age parents, drug addiction, criminal convictions, poverty and violence.

One family's troubles came to a head in February 1979 when a gang of youths wrecked their apartment, sexually molested their 5-year-old son and beat his three brothers and sisters. When a city social worker visited the children's mother after the attack, the mother said the gang had kidnapped her 4-year-old son and was holding him for ransom to be paid from her welfare checks.

A friend told the social worker that the other children could be in danger and that the mother might have emotional problems. The friend later called the social worker to say that the

continued

children had bruises and cigarette burns on their bodies. The kidnapped son was found and was sent to the hospital with burns, bruises and a fever.

The welfare worker checked up on the family in mid-March of that year, but, according to records of the case, the family seemed to have no fixed address between March and December 1979. At one point, the caseworker noted the mother seemed to be unable to protect her children from being beaten by her friends. The caseworker recommended follow-up visits by city officials and counseling for the mother.

In December the social worker reported the mother's friend said the mother was coping well. "As the family is managing, and client isn't asking for any services, we are closing this case," the caseworker recorded.

Just 44 days later, in January 1980, the mother's 15-month-old daughter was dead on arrival at a Brooklyn hospital. The daughter's liver was lacerated and she was bleeding internally. An autopsy showed that the child had old rib fractures and was both undernourished and dehydrated. Investigators found that the daughter had been kicked and hurled against a wall by a man who was living with the mother.

The remaining children, however, were left to live with their mother for nine more months until they were placed in foster homes. The Inspector General's report said the decision to leave the children with their mother was "amazing," especially since the oldest son had witnessed the murder of his sister and later testified against the man, who had not yet been arrested.

"Considering the bizarre and extreme conditions," the report said, "it is incomprehensible that no action was taken to remove these children from such a home environment."

A 6-year-old girl was pronounced dead on arrival at Brookdale Hoapital in Brooklyn on March 2, 1980. Her liver was torn and her spleen was bleeding. Bruises on her body indicated that she had been kicked in the stomach before she died. She also had a scar, shaped like a coat hanger, on her right thigh.

The girl's father was charged with killing her. An investigation showed that he had spent several years in jail for assaults with deadly weapons that included knives, iron pipes and guns.

Four years before her death, the girl and her brother had been placed in foster care with the New York Foundling Hospital because their mother had neglected them. The parents were seperated. The father, who was unemployed, was later jailed for two years for possessing a firearm.

continued

Three-Month Trial Basis

After his release in April 1979, the father took custody of the two children on a three-month trial basis, supporting them on public assistance. The Foundling Hospital asked welfare officials in Brooklyn to monitor the family, and hospital reports showed the family was doing well. Welfare officials recommended extending the trial period.

Then, on Feb. 29, 1980, the children's mother told welfare workers that the father was beating the children and also had failed to clothe and feed them properly. A welfare official tried and failed to visit the father and the children. A broken computer kept the caseworker from searching for an alternative address in public assistance files. Two days later, the girl was dead.

The Inspector General's report criticized welfare officials for not talking with other people who knew the children. A teacher and day-care workers who knew the children later said they had been concerned about how the father was treating the children. The report found "a seriously deficient assessment of the family situation."

Another family came to city welfare workers' attention in January 1974 when their second child was born suffering from drug withdrawal. The girl's mother denied using drugs regularly, but the child's father appears to have been an addict since he agreed to enter a drug therapy program.

The girl was returned to the parents after she recovered from the drug withdrawal. Social workers closed the case in December 1975, "apparently satisfied," the Inspector General said, that the mother and the father were taking care of their children.

Then, in February 1977, city social workers were told that the mother was neglecting her children. The mother had seperated from her husband and moved in with another man. An informant told social workers that they were selling and using heroin. A social worker visited the family and decided that the reports were not substantiated, although the mother admitted to occasional heroin use and heavy drinking.

Three months later, an anonymous source again reported that the mother and the man were using drugs and that the man was beating the mother. The children were also reportedly bruised. A social worker visited the family again but did not feel that the charges were accurate and closed the case.

Used Heroin for Three Years

In October 1977, the mother had a child by the man. The baby also suffered from drug withdrawal. This time the mother admitted having used heroin for three years, and all the children were then placed in foster care.

But in November 1978 a family court returned the children to the mother, even though she had not attended a drug therapy program that she was enrolled in and had not made strong efforts to make a home for the children, the report said.

City social workers lost track of the family after September 1979, but located the family again in January 1980 after receiving a report that the mother was neglecting her children. A social worker found the children in an apartment without electricity or furniture. They were poorly clothed and had not been fed for days. The social worker placed them in foster care again.

A month later, the mother gave birth to a fourth child who was also suffering from drug addiction. Two months later, the mother died; the cause of death is not given in the report.

The Inspector General faulted city social workers for not monitoring the family more closely. "Each of the parents had a history of lying about themselves and each other which made whatever they said questionable," the Inspector General said. "In spite of this, the caseworkers relied primarily on information obtained from the parents in making case decisions."

A 15-year-old girl, still living with her mother and five children, had a baby. Six months later, in October 1976, the grandmother called city social workers to say that her daughter was not caring for the baby. The grandmother threatened to abandon the baby in the hallway unless the city placed the child in foster care.

After a visit to the family, a social worker reported that the grandmother was indifferent to her daughter and grandchild but that they were in no immediate danger.

Three days later, the baby's mother made an emergency visit to the Brooklyn office of the Special Services for Children agency and asked that she and her child be moved away immediately. She said the grandmother drank too much and was abusive.

Separate Foster Programs

The caseworker suggested that the girl try to work things out with her mother. But two and a half weeks later the girl again asked for emergency placement for herself and her baby, and in December 1976 they were placed in separate foster programs.

In January 1977, the baby's mother left foster care and asked to take her child and move in with her sister. City social workers approved of the arrangement. But six months later the baby was placed in foster care again after the sister said the child was being

continued

neglected. In the next week, the mother visited the Brooklyn welfare office four times, begging for her baby to be returned to her.

On the last visit, the grandmother accompanied her and promised to take care of the baby. Social workers disagreed on whether to approve this and asked the child's mother to take an emergency psychiatric examination. The psychiatrist said the teen-ager could have the baby with her, but only if the grandmother had primary responsibility for the child.

So, in August 1977, the family was reunited. Within a week, city social workers closed the case after four unannounced visits showed the family to be coping well. In May 1978, however, the young mother returned to the Brooklyn welfare office, saying that she was overwhelmed.

But the case was not reopened, the Inspector General said, because the grandmother was told that she was responsible for the baby's care.

Bruises and Scars

A year and and half later, in November 1979, Brooklyn Jewish Hospital reported that the baby had been brought in with bruises and scars on the face, one hand and both legs.

A social worker visited the family the next day and found that the teen-ager had had another baby and had moved in with her boyfriend. The grandmother said her daughter neglected the children but did not abuse them.

A week later, the grand-mother and her other daughter asked the city social workers to help the teen-ager because she was unable to take care of the children.

In November 1979, the youngest baby was placed in foster care, while the grand-mother agreed to take the older child. But since the children's mother and her boyfriend said they were eager to have the children back, social workers kept in touch with them and helped them get furniture for their apartment to accommodate the children.

In March 1980, the children were returned to the girl, and in May 1980, the case was closed.

A year later, the Police Department told social workers that both of the children had been badly burned by scalding water. The Inspector General's report does not explain how. The youngest child died the same day. The older child died two weeks later.

The Inspector General's report faulted social workers for not recognizing the seriousness of the problems that the family faced.

"Although the children were placed temporarily several

continued

times," it said, "no thought or effort was given to assist this teen-age mother to develop parenting skills or provide homemaking services in order that she could better manage her responsibilities."

—SOURCE: James Le Moyne, "Child-abuse Cases: Broken Homes, Teen-age Parents, Drugs, and Death. The New York Times, May 1, 1984. pp. B1ff.

REFERENCES

Babbie, E. (1979). *The practice of social research.* Belmont, CA: Wadsworth Publishing Co.

Brody, J. (1979, August 1). Personal health. *The New York Times,* p. C4.

Brody, J. (1981, October 28). Personal health. *The New York Times,* p. C8.

Day, P. (1977). *Methods of learning communication skills.* New York: Pergamon Press.

Gilbert, N., Miller, H., & Specht, H. (1980). *An introduction to social work practice* (chap. 3). Englewood Cliffs, NJ: Prentice-Hall.

Good Tracks, J. (1973). Native American non-interference. *Social Work,* 18 (6), 30-35.

Landy, D. (1965). Problems of persons seeking help in our culture. In Zald, M. (Ed.), *Social welfare institutions* (pp. 559-574). New York: Wiley.

MacNair, R., Wodarski, J. S., & Giordano, J. (1982). Social assessment instrumentation: the implications for delivery of human services. *Arete,* 7 (2), 11-24.

McQuail, D. (1975). *Communication.* New York: Longman Inc.

Morgan, K. (1980). *Children of strangers.* Philadelphia: Temple University Press.

Pincus, A., & Minahan, A. (1973). *Social work practice: Model and method.* Itasca, IL: Peacock Publishers.

Rogers, B., Doron, A., & Jones, M. (1979). *The study of social policy: A comparative approach.* London: Allen & Unwin.

Sauber, S.R. (1983). *The human services delivery system.* New York: Columbia University Press.

Spingarn, N. D. (1982, December 26). Primary nurses bring back one-to-one care. *New York Times Magazine,* pp. 26ff.

Wilson, S. (1978). *Confidentiality in social work.* New York: The Free Press.

Williams, W., & Elmore, R. (Eds.). (1976). *Social program implementation.* New York: Academic Press.

Zastrow, C. (1981). *The practice of social work.* Homewood, IL: Dorsey Press.

INDEX